COLOR YOUR LIFE HAPPY

Create Your Unique Path and Claim the Joy You Deserve

Flora Morris Brown, Ph.D.

Second Edition

Color Your Life Happy:
Create Your Unique Path and Claim the Joy You Deserve
Second Edition

Flora Morris Brown, Ph.D.
Sonata Press
5753-G Santa Ana Canyon Road, #360
Anaheim Hills, CA 92807

Editor: Barbara Ardinger
Book Therapist: Shaun Griffen
Copyeditor: Lynette Smith
Cover Design: TLC Graphics
Author services: Pedernales Publishing, LLC.
www.pedernalespublishing.com

Book Information: http://coloryourlifehappy.com

Brown, Flora Morris.

Color your life happy : create your unique path and claim the joy you deserve / Flora Morris Brown. -- Second edition. -- Anaheim Hills, CA: Sonata Press, [2015]

pages : illustrations ; cm.

ISBN: 978-0-9772183-1-8 (print) ; 0-9772183-1-7 (print) ;
978-0-9772183-0-1 (ebook)
Revises the 2009 edition published by Aviva.
Includes bibliographical references and index.

Summary: This guide reveals skills and tools to help you create a happier life amidst stress and adversity. Practical advice and powerful insights are drawn from positive psychology, teachings from seekers of spiritual enlightenment, and inspiring relatable stories.--Publisher.

1. Happiness. 2. Joy. 3. Self-actualization (Psychology) 4. Success. 5. Quality of life. 6. Conduct of life. 7. Self-acceptance. 8. Self- realization. 9. Self-esteem. 10. Work-life balance. 11. Well-being. 12. Positive psychology. 13. Attitude (Psychology) 14. Change (Psychology) 15. Mental health. I. Title.

BF575.H27 B76 2015 2014902965
158.1--dc23 1508

Disclaimer

Before we dive into the tips, advice, and anecdotes on happiness, let me gently inform you, in case you suffer from clinical depression or other clinical mental diagnoses, that the contents of this book, including text, graphics, and other material, are inspirational and should not be considered or used as a replacement for professional medical or mental health advice, diagnosis, or treatment.

The contents are solely the opinion of the author based on the summary of research, highlights of self-help literature, and personal experiences. None of the contents should be considered as a form of therapy, advice, direction, and/or diagnosis or treatment of any kind: medical, spiritual, psychological, or other.

While the author and publisher have made every effort to use sources we believe to provide reliable information, we also recognize that psychological science, trends, and suggested solutions change. We urge the reader to consult current research, policies, and findings. We have included sources that were current at the time of publication, but

CONTENTS

To Edna and Lewis Cole, who dedicated their lives to helping me and the rest of the members of the Central Youth Council steer clear of danger, make good choices, and still have fun during our adolescent years; to my niece, Mildred Wafford, my number one fan; to my children, Tamra, Sonya, Herbert III, and Adrienne, for tolerating another one of Mom's creative projects; and to my grandchildren, Jasmine, Victor Jr., and Anthony, for their unconditional love.

ACKNOWLEDGEMENTS

I have many people to thank for helping me reach decisions about this book in its various stages over several years.

Thanks to my walking buddy and neighbor, Sonja Grewal, for tolerating how I often turned our banter into discussions about the content, cover, and subtitle of this book. We can finally go back to discussing the flowers that line our walking trail and how, if only given the chance, we would rule the world.

Deep thanks to my developmental editor, Barbara Ardinger, for carefully editing my manuscript and pointing out without hesitation areas that needed rethinking, reworking, and alas, relegating to another project.

I am very appreciative to my book therapist, Shaun Griffen, who helped me achieve clarity, coherence, and fact presentation, as she gently coaxed my message out of my head and into the book.

Thank you Martin Coffee for going through my manuscript with a new set of eyes and suggesting valuable improvements.

To my friend and copyeditor, Lynette Smith, thank you for your patient and thoughtful responses to my many questions about content and structure. Most of all, I'm grateful for your expert attention to my spelling, grammar, punctuation, word choice, and style.

Thank you, Tamara Devers at TLC Graphics, for your patience and talent in creating the perfect cover to convey my book's message.

Thank you, Jose Ramirez at Pedernales Publishing, for your keen eye for detail in design layout and submissions to distribution channels.

Big thank yous to Carol Brown, Gladys Anderson, Melissa Guzzetta, Linda Luke, Melanie Kissell, Shirley George Frazier, and other friends and colleagues who are still talking to me in spite of how often I bugged them for years by email, phone, and in person about the content, design, and other decisions about this book.

INTRODUCTION

"Claim your joy! Don't let anyone steal your joy!" Joel Osteen, senior pastor of the Lakewood Church in Houston, Texas, repeated to punctuate his televised sermon one Sunday morning in 2007.

I was worshipping from bed, as my friend Alice liked to call it whenever we played hooky from church and watched a televised sermon instead, to lessen any feelings of guilt.

As I adjusted a pile of pillows against the headboard to prop myself just right, I reflected on Joel's message. My eyes drifted to a promotional product catalog on my bed that had fallen open to a page showing a box of crayons. I had recently retired from teaching and for days before had been looking for a product I could get personalized to help promote my speaking gigs.

Just as Joel was repeating "Claim your own joy!" again, I blurted out loud, "That's right, ***we must learn to color our lives happy. God has already given us the crayons.***"

Suddenly, Joel's message and the idea of the box of

crayons collided in my mind, firing off the serendipitous phrase *Color Your Life Happy*.

The phrase rang in my ears for a few minutes, feeling deliciously right and perfect for something, although I didn't know what. Then I remembered the Internet gurus' suggesting you buy the domain for any phrase that seemed catchy and could possibly be used later for a product or project.

That spurred me to dash online to see if the domain coloryourlifehappy.com was available.

It was. I bought it without a plan for how I would use it.

Color Your Life Happy began as a blog where I answered the questions people often asked me about how I accomplished this or that in my life. I shared steps and strategies that worked for me. Even though my life didn't seem remarkable to me, I shared advice on making choices that lead to a happier life.

Then in 2008, when I realized that I had written over 100 blog posts, I decided to fashion those posts into a book. The timing was perfect. A new field of positive psychology was engaged in research on the science of happiness, popular TV shows like Oprah featured segments on the search for happiness, inner peace, and the power of thought, college courses on becoming happier sprang up, "happiness" began to show up in fast food slogans, and corporate leaders began to report that happy employees made for happy customers, which of course increased profits.

After publishing the first edition of *Color Your Life Happy* in 2009, however, something didn't sit right about it. Although it enjoyed a modest following and offered some useful advice, I had a desire to go deeper. I became concerned that I had skimmed the surface of my own life experiences and had given some readers the impression that in spite of being raised at a time when African Americans were denied many opportunities, I had somehow been "lucky." Or worse, I worried that readers may have gotten the notion that happiness meant avoiding sadness, grief, adversity, and anger.

In this second edition, along with still sharing some of the leading thoughts on happiness, I have delved deeper into some of the times when I worked through my own sadness, grief, and adversity. I clearly remember feeling in my mid-forties that I was giving more to others than I was to myself. I was a super mom and wife, but feeling neglected and empty. You couldn't tell from the outside because I was raised to put on a happy face.

But one day I decided I wanted my insides to match my outsides. I posted a note on the dashboard of my car: *It's my turn.* Although I don't call it "luck," I had been fortunate enough to have enjoyed some success in my life up to that point. Now I wanted to discover better ways to deal with feelings I was raised to deny, ignore, or mask—and even discuss them in public. (Gasp!)

What got me from there to here was learning to enjoy my own company, loving myself, and having a ready toolkit of healthy ways to deal with the inevitable sad, disappointing, and upsetting times in my life. I grew to trust my intuition, listen to people who were placed in my life to help me and, based on the choices I made, create my unique path.

You may have picked up this book not so much to be happy, but because you are just not satisfied with the way your life is going. Maybe you are ready to say, "It's my turn."

Perhaps you want to make a change in your life, but something is holding you back. You may even feel guilty for wanting a better life. Do you feel stuck in an unsatisfactory job or troubled marriage? You may be ready to dive into a career you've neglected, write a book, learn to fly, or travel the world living out of your suitcase. For many of us, this urge or longing to make a change doesn't go away; it just gets stronger as we grow older.

If you don't allow this longing a positive expression in your life, your frustrated energy can turn inward and fester until you sink into bitterness, resentfulness, and prolonged sadness. Or worse, you could die unfulfilled. You can avoid this fate by taking small steps toward the life you were born to live.

Like you, I scan books, pausing here and there to read sections that jump out at me while deciding whether I am going to plunk down my hard-earned money. If you decide to invest your money and time in *Color Your Life Happy,* here is what I promise.

- You won't be expected to do a major life overhaul to increase your happiness.

- You will be discouraged from trying to be perfect.
- You will be encouraged to accept your flaws and imperfections.
- You will not have to read the whole book if you don't want to (but I hope you do). While there is a logical order to the book, it doesn't have a plot like you'll find with a novel. You can flip to any page and find something helpful there.
- You will discover that if you don't let yourself feel and work through sadness and fear, you won't be able to experience joy either. If this capability weren't already within you, there would be no hope you'd ever manifest it. Thankfully, it is already there!
- You will discover what's holding you back from claiming your own joy. It isn't your fault if you haven't yet realized your own power to color your life happy. Most of us were raised to accept the status quo and do what we were told, without question—first from our parents, then from school, then later from the government, our bosses, and in our personal relationships.
- You will begin to discover your mission and your purpose, and you'll begin to learn how to create your unique path.
- You will discover that it's what you think about yourself that matters.
- You will discover that only you can create your unique path.

- You deserve the joy that's waiting for you to claim it.

It's your turn to color your life happy, so go ahead and trust what resonates with you in this book to create your unique path, and without hesitation and apology, claim the joy you deserve.

Opening Your Mind to Happiness

Happiness is when what you think, what you say, and what you do are in harmony.

—Mahatma Gandhi

We were raised to smile on cue, my two sisters and I. When my mother pulled out her Kodak Brownie camera and posed us in front of our house or church, we knew to break out into full-toothed smiles. Look happy. *Snap*. An outward show of unhappiness was just not allowed.

My sisters and I were just a few years apart. I was the oldest, Sonja was one year younger, and Mildred was one and a half years younger than Sonja.

What, my mother asked, did we have to be unhappy about? After all, we didn't have polio, the most feared childhood ailment of the '50s, and we had clothes, shelter, and more food than the starving children in foreign countries.

Mother's exhortations worked for the most part, except for my middle sister, Sonja, who looked quite unhappy in almost every childhood photo. If digital cameras had been invented back then, I can imagine my mother previewing every shot and, upon discovering the frown, taking the shots over and over until she got the happy family photo she wanted.

No one ever thought to investigate why my sister always seemed unhappy. She could have been depressed, but that was not a word I recall hearing during my childhood. "She's just like my sister Ida," my father said many times. That diagnosis, which was never explained, stuck. Although I never met any of my father's relatives, I guess Aunt Ida must have been unhappy. Or at least she didn't smile on cue.

In the 1950s, most of the adults around me didn't seem concerned about the emotional and psychological states of children. Parents could exact whatever punishment they wanted on their children without fear of the authorities. Even God was in on it, according to the way adults interpreted the Bible:

> *Train up a child in the way he should go, And when he is old he will not depart from it.*
>
> —Proverbs 22:6 NKJV

Spare the rod, spoil the child.
—A perversion of Proverbs 13:24 NJKV

The last thing any right-thinking '50s parent wanted was a spoiled child, so they held back on praise while they emphasized proper behavior and looking happy. Children of color had an additional burden. Not only did we have to stay in the proper child's place, but we also had to stay on our side of the racial divide, where being overtly angry or unhappy in public was frowned upon from both sides of the track.

Feeling sad? "Wipe those tears away," adults told us, "or I'll give you something to cry about." That was bad advice. I've since learned that tears can be very cleansing.

Long before spiritual leaders and psychologists promoted the idea that we create our own happiness, I had already discovered that any chance I had to survive a '50s childhood was in my own hands.

Call me a Pollyanna. Call me a Miss Goody Two-Shoes. Or a wimp. My goals were to do what led to praise and happy outcomes and to avoid doing anything that brought punishment and pain—especially anything that brought on my mother's wrath.

Don't get me wrong. I spoke up and voiced my strong opinions, but I learned early to pick my battles carefully.

All in all, my childhood was not as bad as some and worlds better than many. Thanks to my mother's smart handling of money, her resourcefulness in seeking out and involving us in positive activities, her skillful cooking and sewing, and her mastery of music (she was a superb pianist and organist), we had a stable and safe routine and home environment. We were always well-groomed from head to toe and often dressed in outfits my mother had created and customized. Reaching back to her Southern roots, she also canned fruit and vegetables for the winter, so we always had nourishing meals.

Still, there was so much emphasis on keeping up appearances, on "being good," that we perhaps did not learn to honor and respect our true feelings, nor learn to express them in appropriate and productive ways—both the socially accepted ones like happiness, and the more difficult ones like anger and fear. As a child, I yearned for real happiness, even though I wasn't exactly sure what it was. My life's work has been to understand that true happiness arises from learning to accept and learn from all our feelings, and from our struggles right alongside our triumphs. I'd love to share with you this journey of discovery, my research, and my work as I've learned to embrace and celebrate life in all its many wondrous and beautiful colors.

Where did our pursuit of happiness begin?

> *The foolish man seeks happiness in the distance; the wise grows it under his feet.*
>
> —James Oppenheim

Even though the pursuit of happiness is America's favorite part of the Declaration of Independence (though they mistakenly interpret its meaning), few people openly admitted what they were doing until the '60s. Before then, being openly happy and cheerful usually meant you were too addle-brained to realize how serious life was. Or you were a hippie twirling in circles in the streets of the famous (or infamous) Haight-Ashbury district in San Francisco, spouting love and peace but doing little to lend respectability to happiness.

In spite of my childhood plan to create real happiness by seeking fun and joy-filled activities while avoiding punishment and pain, I was pretty sure wearing tie-dyed shirts, experimenting with LSD, and living in a commune with wannabe musicians was not the route for me.

Edward Diener (http://diener.socialpsychology.org/) entered uncharted territory in the '70s when he tried to get approval for a study of happiness while he was a graduate student at Fresno State University in California. He had grown up on a farm and believed that farmers were happy. Now he wanted to study their behavior and measure their responses to his questionnaire. But his major professor rejected Ed's first idea; when Ed changed it to a study of conformity—oh, the irony!—his professor approved it.

It wasn't until 1981, when Dr. Diener earned tenure at the University of Illinois, that he was finally free to conduct research on happiness. Even then, however, to ensure that his work would be respected as scientific study, he chose to call his topic *subjective well-being* rather than *happiness*. He still worked in obscurity and was viewed with skepticism by the academic community, which dubbed him Dr. Happiness. Finally, after collaborating with graduate students and colleagues, he succeeded in making the study of happiness a respectable topic of serious academic study. As a distinguished professor of psychology at the University of Illinois, Dr. Ed Diener spent over three decades studying what makes people feel happy.

He learned that people around the world experience "subjective well-being" when their basic needs are met, when they have autonomy, and when they enjoy social support. Happy people tend to make more money, have better social relationships, do more volunteer work, and have better health. Although Abraham Maslow (http://maslow.com/) had created his famous "hierarchy of needs" as early as 1954, psychologists still thought it was just a theory. Diener's research findings applied Maslow's theory to practical situations. His research also confirmed other research that indicates happiness is in part genetically determined. (More on this later.)

I was fortunate to meet Dr. Diener in January 2009 at the Applying the Science of Positive Psychology to Improve Society Conference at the Claremont Graduate University School of Behavioral and Organizational Sciences in California. When I spotted him in the lobby, I couldn't resist telling him that a lot of the findings on positive psychology sounded like what our grandmas always told us. He agreed, but added that people don't pay attention until you measure things scientifically and cite your findings in learned papers.

Happiness research: studying the sunny side

Until Diener's decades of study and research on happiness led to publications on the topic, scientists and psychologists studied *what was wrong* with humans—our physical illnesses, mental illnesses, depression, paranoia, and neurosis, to name a few.

In 1998, when Dr. Martin Seligman (http://www.positivepsychology.org) was named president of the American Psychological Association, he envisioned a new direction for psychology. Instead of just focusing on conditions that caused humans to *flounder*, he wondered what conditions enabled us to *flourish*. When he decided to turn from research emphasizing unhappy states and mental illness to studying people who were happy and content with their lives, his goal was to expand research devoted to happiness. So he raised $1 million and gathered a thousand therapists to create a way to conduct scientific research. Out of their meetings, a new field—positive psychology—was born to build objective evidence of the components of happiness.

Seligman also wanted to call attention to the work of early researchers such as Diener, and he encouraged other psychologists to study the sunny side of the street as well. Since the birth of the field of positive psychology, a growing body of research has sprung into the limelight as the subject of research, classes, books, and TV shows:

- In January 2005, *Time Magazine* devoted an entire issue to research results and articles about happiness.
- In spring 2006, students at Harvard University flocked to a new course, Positive Psychology, led by Tal Ben-Shahar (http://www.talbenshahar.com), in which he taught students on the subject of how to be happy. Over a hundred other colleges followed suit, offering similar courses.
- In 2000, fifty books on happiness were released; in 2008, four thousand books on happiness were published.
- Life coaches sprang up, ready to help you plan a life that leads to your happiness.
- Oprah led the way in promoting the search for happiness on her TV shows and in her magazine. When her show was still on the air, she went on location, for example, to interview residents of areas of the world, such as Denmark, that researchers had identified as the happiest places on earth. Every issue of her website and print magazine still gives tips on living a life that leads to happiness.
- In his book *Delivering Happiness*, CEO of Zappos, Tony Hsieh (2013) shared the business lessons he learned that led to his success. He said, for example, to treat employees right because happy employees make for happy customers.

WHAT IS HAPPINESS?

Happiness has been described in many ways in literature and research: being satisfied with life, being content, and being engaged in fulfilling activities. Happiness is an emotion of inner joy, contentment, and a feeling of well-being. Researchers seem to agree that happy people tend to see the positive side of things, even in pain and tragedy. They see opportunities rather than problems. They make choices that lead to doing what they enjoy, often find pleasure in simple things, and believe in a power greater than themselves. They have close relationships and express gratitude for their lives.

WHAT HAPPINESS IS NOT

Happiness is not the absence of sadness. Quite the contrary. Happy people acknowledge sadness and allow themselves to feel it. They choose to not be crushed by it, but instead learn from it and move beyond it.

Happiness is not the situational emotional high you feel when you win the lottery or get a new car. These are short term. You probably don't get the same thrill from your new car a few months later as you did the day you drove it off the lot.

One of the customers at my manicurist shop had an appointment just before mine every month. She was always cheerful and full of lively conversation. When I'd mention my upcoming vacations, she'd always offer tips on places to visit in the locale because she had already been there. She enjoyed movies, visiting casinos, shopping, and spending time with her many friends and family. She was so much fun I always looked forward to seeing her. You can imagine my shock to learn that she had stage IV cancer and was almost always in physical discomfort and pain from chemotherapy and other invasive treatments. The only time I'd ever seen a hint of sadness in her was the day after her brother died. When I visited her in the hospital a few weeks before she died, she was hooked up to multiple tubes and still, when I walked in her room, she threw open her arms and welcomed me with a big warm smile.

> *It is pretty hard to tell what does bring happiness; poverty and wealth have both failed.*
>
> —Kin Hubbard

How happy are we?

An important piece of research by Bouchard, Lykken, McGue, Segal, and Tellegen (1990) studied the role our genes might play in our sense of satisfaction with our lives. They gathered data on four thousand sets of twins born in Minnesota between 1936 and 1955. Based on their findings, they concluded that 50 percent of our happiness is based on our genetics. What does that mean? If you think some people are just born with a sunny disposition, according to these studies, you are correct.

What does this mean about the rest of us? Eight percent of our happiness can be attributed to the circumstances in our lives, such as our educational level, our marital status, and our income. The remaining 40 percent is a reflection of our attitude or outlook on life. This is the part of our happiness over which we have control.

Research thus indicates that there is much we can do to increase our level of happiness. We'll explore this in upcoming chapters.

Time Magazine reported in its January 2005 issue that 78 percent of Americans were happy most to all of the time, 16 percent were happy some of the time, and 8 percent were seldom happy. Eighty percent said they generally wake up happy. Seventy-five percent considered themselves optimists.

Most Americans believe we live in the greatest country in the world, yet in a report on happiness by Inglehart, Foa, Peterson, and Welzel (2008), we ranked number sixteen. Denmark was at the top of the list, Zimbabwe at the bottom. Based on how the countries ranked in happiness, the presence or restriction of political freedom seems to have had something to do with the respondents' perceptions of happiness.

In a 2013 study of developed nations by the Paris-based Organization for Economic Cooperation and Development (OECD), Australia ranked as Number 1 in happiness, America, No. 6. Health, safety, environment, civic engagement, and housing were among the key factors.

How happy are you?

We live mostly in our heads, and thoughts about the past and the future dominate our waking hours. Price (2009) discovered it's not what others think about us that worries us, but what we *think* others think about us.

Lipton (2007) found that we have a subconscious script that plays in our head. It's made up of what we observed and learned about what our parents thought about us before we were seven years of age. When our conscious minds are not paying attention, we default to this subconscious script, which too often doesn't support self-love. If our subconscious script says we are not smart, for example, and we want to earn a college degree, we have to struggle harder to achieve that goal. He believed that once we become aware of this hidden script, we can reprogram our subconscious.

We're quite skillful at creating drama in our heads. Usually, we're able to control our emotions, but unfortunately too many of us direct our thoughts to things that make us sad or feel pessimistic about the future.

For example, I was driving on the freeway to attend a local weekend reunion with friends I had met in Italy. I decided to use my driving time to call a friend on my cell phone. (Yes, I used my hands-free device.) I began to tell my friend how, in spite of my urging my daughter to travel by air, she had driven alone from Southern California to the Bay Area to attend a conference. As I got into the story, my anxiety about my daughter's trip started to return. Suddenly, I realized that my until-then repressed anxiety was compromising my own safe driving. I had to stop my story immediately and focus on calming, positive thoughts in order to finish my own trip safely.

No one is as good as we are at making ourselves feel scared, anxious, and sad. If that's correct, then couldn't we be just as good at bringing up the opposite emotions? Let's see if this theory could work for positive feelings.

Think of a situation you've enjoyed. Put yourself back there and visualize as many details as possible. Recall how you felt in that situation and bring that feeling back to the surface. Sustain the feeling for as long as possible.

I always feel happy when I think about my visit to St. Mark's Square in the heart of Venice, Italy, one of the most photographed and celebrated destinations in the world. The square is lined with sidewalk cafes and boutiques on three sides and St. Mark's Basilica at the eastern end. As soon as I entered the Square, a flock of pigeons flew overhead and the music of three orchestras filled the night air. I felt like Audrey Hepburn, whom we often saw in movies with her arms stretched out and her head tilted back.

Being able to direct or redirect your thoughts to positive images that bring you joy is an important component of your happiness.

But you're probably thinking, *How can I be happy when there's so much sadness, misery, and turmoil in the world?* Let me ask you this: Can you think of any way in which your worries have stopped wars, fed the hungry, or made the world a better place?

> *Be the change you want to see in the world.*
>
> —Mahatma Gandhi

A few years ago I had dinner with a friend who has been a lawyer for thirty years. He shared an experience he had when he was part of a panel speaking to new lawyers.

One of the young lawyers asked, "What's the best way we can help poor people?"

"By not becoming one of them," my friend fired back.

I laughed at this story, but he was so right.

Many people are compassionate about helping others, but they probably need just as much help themselves. You can't give others what you don't have yourself. If you long to help the poor or anyone else, first be sure you have what you want to give. If you want the world to be a happy place, then you have to be happy first.

If you feel guilty about striving for happiness with so much poverty and violence in the world, note that Lama and Cutler (2009) stressed we should help ourselves and others simultaneously. The research shows the mutual benefit: Happy people tend to be more open to helping others, and helping others makes us happy.

Four problems with the concept of happiness

Human beings have looked for happiness since the beginning of time. We live in the most enlightened and technologically advanced period of history. Why are we still looking for happiness?

1. *We don't seem to know what happiness is.* Most of the ancient Greek philosophers saw happiness not as a matter of luck but as something that could be controlled and increased. In fact, Aristotle's term *eudaimonia* is often translated as "happiness." But actually, the two words are not exactly synonymous.

For Aristotle, *eudaimonia* was an activity of flourishing, living an ethical life. *Eudaimonia* is objective and is based on living not in a search for pleasure, but according to ethics such as courage, temperance, and honesty, engaging in good habits, and living to your fullest potential. If you die in battle to save a comrade, you certainly experienced pain and suffering, but you have achieved *eudaimonia* because you put another's needs above yours. You died with honor. According to Aristotle, then, happiness was the way you lived your life, not the way you felt about your life.

Our modern definition of happiness, however, is subjective. It means different things to each of us. Our practice of seeking pleasure and trying to avoid pain may put us in the hedonic camp of emotions, but many of us also commit to living meaningful lives, similar to Aristotle's eudemonia. The line between these two views of happiness has faded.

Biswas-Diener (https://positiveacorn.com/resources/Brief_History_Eudemonia.pdf) urged us not to rush to believe that one is better than the other, but rather to recognize that both have a place in our modern lives. He also pointed out that happiness research is still in its infancy and is showing that not only can both the eudemonic and hedonic views coexist, but there is much more about happiness to discover.

Much of what we read about happiness assumes that our basic needs have been met and we are ready to master our reactions and attitudes. It was Abraham Maslow (http://www.maslow.com/), father of the humanistic movement, who put the spotlight on basic needs in the 1950s when he turned his (and our) attention from what he saw as a pessimistic view of mankind to a positive view of what motivates us to achieve. He developed his five-stage hierarchy of needs, illustrating his belief that once we fulfill our basic needs of food, shelter, warmth, and sleep, we will feel the need for safety, security, law, protection from the elements, and so on, until we reach the top level. In the 1970s, two new needs were added at the top of Maslow's hierarchy: self-actualization—"finding meaning in your life" and "self-transcendence"—devoting yourself to a higher good, being altruistic.

I agree with Maslow that we can't focus on higher needs until we take care of the bottom of the hierarchy. We see evidence of how needs work when we look at victims of disasters, such as Hurricane Katrina in August 2005. Some survivors of disaster may have been at the top of the hierarchy, but they suddenly lost their homes and feelings of safety. They slid right to the bottom of Maslow's hierarchy of needs as their concern for survival became paramount. The day before such a disaster, folks at the self-actualization level may have been registering for a personal growth workshop. The day after the disaster, as victims of the destruction, they were no longer concerned with personal growth, but with finding a safe place to live, keeping warm, and finding food to eat.

Can we live a happy life even if, for example, our idea of happiness is brutalizing people for fun? Or does happiness apply only to those of us who lead good and ethical lives? If so, who gets to decide what's good and what's ethical?

Some modern psychologists have solved this dilemma, at least for themselves, by insisting that we shouldn't mix ethics with our self-reported feelings about the quality of our life. I believe, however, that true happiness must be a combination of state of mind and how we handle the inevitable adversities of our lives.

Gore (2010) discovered an ever bigger problem with happiness. The research supporting the new positive psychology was being conducted by men, while the criticism of it was often being offered by women. Disturbed that some experts were convinced women who lived traditionally married lives were happier than those with feminist values, she conducted her own interview of hundreds of women. Her insights helped balance the happiness discussion. She discovered that throughout history psychology has failed women repeatedly [as it has ethnic minorities] by insisting we do what is expected of us and discounting our right to go after the lives we really want. She urged women to create a liberation psychology where they could make their own decisions, follow their own dreams, and embrace joy.

2. *We don't know what makes us happy.* Have you ever found yourself standing in line at a fast food restaurant, staring at the menu, unable to decide what to order? You study the menu as if there's going to be a test until the cashier urges you to step aside for the customers behind you who know what they want.

Happiness is like that. You have to know what you want—what makes you happy—before you can have it. Dyer (2005) pointed out that we often focus on what we don't want and then wonder why we get it.

Kant (http://plato.stanford.edu/entries/kant) believed

that duty and moral law are more important than happiness. He found that if happiness is the ultimate aim of life, then we should have only instincts, not reason. We constantly seek something we think will make us happy, but that feeling lasts for only a short time. Eventually, we look for something else.

Scientists believe not knowing what makes us happy stems from a primitive part of the brain that dooms us to the "hedonic treadmill," a term coined by Brickman and Campbell (1971). They found that once we get what we long for, that which makes us excited or happy, then we get used to it and return to a neutral level of emotion. We repeat this jump and fall again and again by going after something else new, only to end up back at the same place each time. We adapt to whatever gave us a burst of happiness, with increased happiness always just out of our reach.

More recent research reveals that we return to our own level of happiness or set points, not to a neutral level. These set points differ individually and can be raised or lowered by how we choose to live our lives. The saying that "happiness is a journey, not a destination" gets to the heart of how we can change our happiness level. Enjoying the experience, the ups and downs of getting what we want, will ensure our happiness. If we don't enjoy the journey, we are destined to look back at our lives lamenting, like Peggy Lee in the song, "Is that all there is?"

We can also overthink happiness. Gruber (2011)

and other researchers believe that when we dwell on being happier and closely monitor our feelings, we can experience the opposite result. Even when we feel good, we may worry that we should be happier.

Gilbert (2005) reported we are woefully inadequate at predicting how we will feel when we get what we want: We exaggerate how we felt in the past and overestimate how we'll feel in the future; we rely on observing what others have done. That can be okay, as long as we realize that there will be details we can't anticipate.

To avoid being caught on the hedonic treadmill or dooming ourselves to perpetual dissatisfaction with our level of happiness, I like to take the advice of Dyer (2005) to go after what we want, but not be attached to the outcome. In other words, I certainly would love to win the lottery, but it would be foolish to become morose because I wasn't holding the winning ticket. (More about money and happiness later.)

3. *We aren't sure we even want happiness.* Unhappiness is more comfortable and socially acceptable than happiness. Sounds strange, doesn't it? In spite of all the books, television talk shows, and marketing experts that tell us how to be happy, we still hold happiness in low regard.

Ernest Hemingway expressed the way many people feel when he said, "Happiness in intelligent people is the rarest thing I know."

We don't want to be seen as Pollyannas who shut our eyes to the "real" world or as clueless dullards who aren't sharp enough to see the harsh realities of life, so we wrestle with the conflicting desires of secretly wanting happiness for ourselves, but publicly showing disdain for it.

How happy are you? Want to find out? Visit Dr. Seligman's website, http://www.authentichappiness.com/, to develop insights into yourself and the world around you. Learn about yourself by taking free, scientifically tested questionnaires, surveys, and scales covering such areas as compassion, overall happiness, character strengths, and close relationships.

4. ***Happiness requires making efforts and taking risks.*** Although we all enjoy watching Olympic medalists as they compete to win top honors in their sports, few of us would be willing to put in the years of training and make the sacrifices these superstars make.

We pay lip service to happiness, but when it comes to putting in the effort to make the changes or take the steps suggested by books, therapists, researchers, and spiritual leaders, many of us just take the easy way out and stay where we are.

In the movie *Sudden Impact*, Clint Eastwood's Dirty Harry character perhaps sums it up best when he says, "Everybody wants results, but nobody wants to do what it takes to get them."

Kashdan and Biswas-Diener (2014) offered a more balanced view when they urged us to avoid labeling negative emotions as bad. They used the results of research to reveal that negative emotions are an unappreciated resource and part of our overall healthy makeup. By being aware and appreciative of what we often think of as our dark side, and handling these inevitable experiences, we build our resilience and open the way to greater joy.

When we encounter discomfort and feel negative emotions, we must look for the information they offer and use it to take positive action. At the same time, we must not obsess over pursuing happiness or overthinking it to the point where we diminish positive experiences and interfere with the very success we seek.

No one person has all the answers. We all view life differently, based on our experiences and perceptions, much like the six blind men of Indostan in the poem by John Godfrey Saxe. When each blind man is asked to describe an elephant, he describes the animal based on the part of the animal he is touching. Not one of them describes the elephant in its entirety.

The Blind Men and the Elephant

by John Godfrey Saxe

It was six men of Indostan
To learning much inclined,
Who went to see the Elephant
(Though all of them were blind),
That each by observation
Might satisfy his mind

The First approached the Elephant,
And happening to fall
Against his broad and sturdy side,

At once began to bawl:
"God bless me! but the Elephant
Is very like a wall!"

The Second, feeling of the tusk,
Cried, "Ho! what have we here
So very round and smooth and sharp?
To me 'tis mighty clear
This wonder of an Elephant
Is very like a spear!"

The Third approached the animal,
And happening to take
The squirming trunk within his hands,
Thus boldly up and spake:
"I see," quoth he, "the Elephant
Is very like a snake!"

The Fourth reached out an eager hand,
And felt about the knee.
"What most this wondrous beast is like
Is mighty plain," quoth he;
"'Tis clear enough the Elephant
Is very like a tree!"

The Fifth, who chanced to touch the ear,
Said: "E'en the blindest man
Can tell what this resembles most;
Deny the fact who can
This marvel of an Elephant
Is very like a fan!"

The Sixth no sooner had begun
About the beast to grope,
Then, seizing on the swinging tail
That fell within his scope,
"I see," quoth he, "the Elephant
Is very like a rope!"

And so these men of Indostan
Disputed loud and long,
Each in his own opinion
Exceeding stiff and strong,
Though each was partly in the right,
And all were in the wrong!

Moral:
So oft in theologic wars,
The disputants, I ween,
Rail on in utter ignorance
Of what each other mean,
And prate about an Elephant
Not one of them has seen!

The poem, which is based on an Indian fable, shows how what we perceive can lead to some serious misinterpretations. Just as each blind man only touched one part of the elephant, so do we only experience one part of reality. And like the blind men in the poem, we draw conclusions about the whole based on our limited and inadequate information. But unlike the blind men in the poem, we can intentionally expand our observations, knowledge, and relationships and use what we learn to make choices we believe will result in our happiness.

Summary

While human beings have always searched for happiness, modern scientists and psychologists have recently begun to reexamine and redefine happiness in many settings and cultures.

They (and we) have learned that our efforts to create happy lives are thwarted by several things. We aren't sure whether happiness is a feeling of pleasure, a way of living, or just getting the things we want.

Sometimes, when we focus on what we *think* we want, we find ourselves distracted by thoughts of what we *don't* want or what others *say* we should want. Because we attract what we think about, it's urgent that we think about what we want, not what we don't want. But this isn't as easy as it sounds. We seem drawn to what's negative and are suspicious of what's good. Many of us even think it's selfish to want to be happy.

Although traditional and modern psychology failed women repeatedly by its male-driven emphasis that women are happiest when they do what is expected of them, growing research debunks this flawed thinking.

Instead of hiding from inevitable negative emotions and labeling them as bad, we all gain strength by working through them and thereby increase our capacity for joy.

Research with happy people has revealed they share some common traits.

- Practice positive attitude.
- Show gratitude.
- Build close relationships with friends and family.
- Work at something they enjoy.
- Believe in something bigger than themselves.
- Have a willingness to forgo momentary happiness to take risks that lead to greater psychological highs.

Creating a happier life requires you to believe in happiness and open your mind to the possibility of a happy life. To experience happiness you must also feel and learn from the negative emotions that arise and take positive action as a result. When you accept that you have the right to joy, you have moved closer to claiming it.

> Color your life *alive* with plenty of sunshine. Lack of sunshine contributes to depression.

HAPPINESS FLASHBACK

When we were preparing to move to a new house, I asked my youngest daughter, Adrienne, then seven years old, to sort the silverware. I wanted her to put aside any pieces that weren't part of a set so I could donate them to charity. When I checked on her progress, she pointed to the potential discards and said, "Mommy, here are all the ones without friends."

Preparing Your Mind for Happiness

What you think of yourself is much more important than what others think of you.

—Lucius Annaeus Seneca

My view of a happy life was shaped by the movies, the conversations the customers had in my mother's beauty shop, and church activities during the week and on Sundays.

Every Saturday, my father took us to the movies at the Criterion Theater on Franklin Avenue in St. Louis while my mother worked in her home-based beauty shop, pressing and curling her customers' hair. We must have seen every new release in the late '40s through the '50s. John Wayne's movies and *The Barefoot Contessa*. The grand musicals like *The King and I*, *Oklahoma*, and *South Pacific*. The romantic comedies starring Rock Hudson and Doris Day.

A few of the movies even had black casts, like *Carmen Jones*, starring Dorothy Dandridge and Harry Belafonte, and *Cabin in the Sky*, starring nearly all the major African-American stars of the 1940s—Ethel Waters, Lena Horne, Eddie "Rochester" Anderson, Rex Ingram, Louis Armstrong, and Duke Ellington.

For me, these movies were more than escape. They were instructional. Watching them, I dreamed about the future. I would have a dining room table with six chairs, and it would be set with beautiful linens and shiny dishes and candles. There would be soft carpeting on my floors, and I would dance around my kitchen. Best of all, my bathroom would be awe-inspiring with its matching towels, fragrant soap, and lots of light.

At the movies, I dreamed that I would avoid the troubled love affairs and money problems that so often were central to the stories on the screen, especially the ones with the all-black casts.

By the time I was thirteen, I had decided on names for my future children. They were all based on the movies. My first son would be Derek, after John Derek, the good-looking American actor I saw in *Rogues of Sherwood Forest*. My first daughter would be named Desiree after the lead character in the 1954 historical movie *Désirée*, starring Jean Simmons and Marlon Brando.

I wrote those names down over and over, adding the surname of whatever guy I was in love with at the time. All my friends knew those names since I also talked about them nonstop at church, school, and home.

Like some of the other naïve ideas I concocted, this one didn't turn out as planned. Both my sisters had children before I finished college and got married, and they snagged my cherished names without warning. My sister Mildred took the name Derek for her first son, and my sister Sonja named her first daughter Desiree. I was deeply hurt that they stole my future children's names. Everyone *knew* those names were mine! Later, however, I managed to find names for my four children: Tamra, Sonya, Herbert III, and Adrienne.

Years later, when I asked my sisters why they'd "stolen" the names I was set on, they said they thought I would be an old maid school teacher and never need those names at all. Thank goodness the old maid image my sisters held for me was nothing like the image I held for myself as a wife and mother in my imagined happy future life.

The beauty shop

While I was learning the way I wanted my life to be from the movies, I also began shaping what I *didn't want* by eavesdropping on my mother and her customers in the beauty shop.

Like it or not, beauticians are drawn into the role of therapist. My mother's customers shared their problems, sought advice, and even asked her to keep money they were hiding from their husbands.

I listened for hours to the women as they shared their woes, and then I also listened to the gossip about those same women. I was a child. They all ignored me. As I grew up, though, they expelled me from the room. I had to listen through the walls.

From listening to the lives of my mother's customers as they postponed their happiness, I decided I would

- Value myself enough to realize that any occasion can be special and I can enjoy my home and possessions, rather than save them for imagined special occasions that may never come, like some of the women who came to my mother's beauty shop.
- Take good care of myself while I was taking care of my kids.
- Follow my educational goals.
- Never settle for less than I thought I deserved.

While many of the women in the beauty shop had their share of problems with husbands and money, they were always very supportive of me and encouraged me and my sisters. They praised me when I showed off my report card, they donated to school and church fundraisers, and they gave us tips when we ran errands for them (although my mother frowned on our accepting money for running errands). Best of all, the beauty-shop women encouraged my early entrepreneurial efforts by buying the handmade potholders and other crafts I peddled in the shop.

At church

Every Sunday, my mother took us to church while our father stayed at home. We started with Sunday school at 9:30 a.m., then went to the 11 a.m. service. We went home for dinner and returned to the church for Baptist Training Union (which was like Sunday school), followed by the Sunday-night service.

If I learned about what I wanted at the movies and what I didn't want from the beauty-shop women, at church I learned what was possible for my life. The Central Baptist Church was nothing like what people expected in a Baptist church. Our pastor, Dr. Thomas E. Huntley, delivered intellectual lectures, rather than the emotional, Bible-thumping sermons that folks heard in most Baptist churches. He had written several books, traveled the world, and nurtured relationships with up-and-coming ministers and politicians. I remember hearing Martin Luther King, Jr. speak at our church long before he answered the call to lead the civil rights movement.

Many of our church leaders were highly educated and were teachers or administrators in the St. Louis school system. My pastor held a Ph.D. My high school principal was a church trustee and also held a Ph.D. Other members of my church were my elementary school nurse and her husband, who was the vice principal at school and the superintendent of Sunday school at church.

I was very impressed and inspired by these church leaders. Not only did I love the way they spoke and carried themselves, but I also admired them. They dressed well, owned cars, and lived in brick homes on the west side of town. I was sure education would enable me to enjoy a similar lifestyle. Once I asked one of my church leaders what was the highest college degree you could earn. When he said Ph.D., I immediately added that to the list of things I wanted for my life.

We had four choirs: the children's choir, the Treblettes; the preteen choir, The Treble Choir; the young adult choir; and the choir to which we all aspired, the Chancel Choir.

The members of the Chancel Choir were highly accomplished vocalists who performed the beautiful compositions of Handel, Saint-Saëns, and Bach and cantatas like *The Seven Last Words* and Handel's *Messiah*, along with Negro spirituals like *Steal Away to Jesus* and *Swing Low, Sweet Chariot*. After listening to the adults sing those songs for many years, I made my way from the children's choir to the youth choir and eventually into the Chancel Choir.

The sacred songs I first learned at church continued to be part of the repertoire that I sang in high school and university choirs. To this day, my love of music continues to be a source of comfort and joy in my life, a wonderful and fulfilling way to express deep feelings, and a definite contributor to my happiness.

From watching the actors in the movies, the real-life characters that came through my life in my mother's beauty shop, and the members of my childhood church, I saw that happiness was not simple. I began to realize that no matter how life appears on the outside, or how much we plan our lives, horrible things sometimes happen.

I was horrified, for example, when one of my favorite Sunday school teachers was shot by her estranged husband outside the church one Sunday just after services had ended. Thankfully, my mother, my sisters, and I had already headed home before this tragedy occurred, and thus we missed being eyewitnesses to this horror.

Another time, one of the boys in the children's choir climbed on top of the elevator car in his apartment building and was crushed when it reached the top floor. The children's choir sang at his funeral. I prayed over and over again that God would keep this from happening to my daredevil sister, Mildred. It was the first time I knew someone my own age who had died. I also remember when fourteen-year-old Emmet Till was lynched in 1955 for allegedly whistling at a white clerk in a Mississippi grocery store.

It is so much easier to have an upbeat attitude when you have a good income, live a life of privilege, and have had no tragedies in your family. I struggle with the New Age idea that we *attract* the bad things that happen to us. Who in their right minds would choose homelessness, depression, sickness, and tragedy?

And yet that is exactly what we seem to do in so many instances.

I think there are many ways in which we yield to societal pressures that result in sabotaging our plans and indeed attracting unwanted experiences into our lives.

I think there are more complicated societal pressures at work in many instances, and that it's against these that we need to direct our attention. Although we will face life's injustices and adversities, it's worthwhile to aim for attracting good works and like-minded compassionate people into our lives. A fundamental tension in traditional and nontraditional religion is the attempt to explain why horrible things happen, especially when we can't pinpoint a direct cause. Kushner (2004) explained that life's events are random, not punishment from an angry God or our just desserts for being bad people. His belief is that asking, "Why did this or that happen to me?" is the wrong question because it seeks to blame and focus on the past. Instead, Kushner said that we should ask, "What can I do now?" and focus on what we can do in the present.

What I have learned is that being happy doesn't mean I will be spared from having upsetting things happen in my life. Also, I don't have to be fake and pretend that all is well when it isn't. I can be sad, upset, and downright disgusted, and still return to my baseline level of happiness. In fact, if we can't be sad or unhappy, we can't be happy. Not being able to feel a range of emotions means we are stuck or numb.

If your happiness meter is stuck at moody, cranky, negative, judgmental, and just plain miserable, then you can't expect to jump into happiness overnight. That would be a tremendous shock to your system. It's probably scary to think about being happy—or even to think happiness is attainable. After all, you're comfortable and familiar with being unhappy. You've invested a lot of time in cultivating it. But if you're going to become happy, then you're going to have to step out of your comfort zone. *Brrr!*

You're going to have to come to terms with the fact that being unhappy is popular. Complaining about everything that's wrong with the world can fill hours of conversation with friends and even perfect strangers. Complaining seems to bind us together in some type of collective misery.

Besides, the whole news industry feeds on sadness, tragedy, war, conflict, and upset.

Being happy is not for the faint-hearted. It takes courage and energy to move from one way of thinking to another or from one set of habits to another. Your happiness can also worry others around you.

For example, a member of my church stopped me one day and asked, "Are you always happy?"

"What do you mean?" I responded, feeling almost guilty for a moment.

"You're always smiling," he replied.

"Well, yes, I am happy most of the time," I stammered. For some reason, I was too chicken to answer with an unqualified yes.

So let me warn you. If you go around smiling, humming a happy song, or uttering cheery "good mornings" to everyone, then you may come under some unwarranted suspicion and scrutiny. Some grouchy people will think you're either daft or just too stupid to realize that life is too serious to go around smiling all the time. You'll intimidate other people. They'll think your happiness means your life is perfect. It won't even occur to them to understand that you've chosen how you will react to the sad and unhappy incidents in your life. And you'll also run into people who will be jealous of you. After all, how dare you be happy when they aren't? Finally, you may even be ridiculed by the insecure people around you. Yes, consider yourself forewarned.

Before you can become happier, more successful, or achieve your new goal, you need to be prepared for these reactions from the people in your world.

What's wrong with rose-colored glasses?

My efforts to remain positive have led to my being accused of "seeing the world through rose-colored glasses." Seeing the world through rose-colored glasses means you have a positive outlook on life, even when circumstances don't seem to warrant it. It frequently implies that the wearer of said glasses is gullible, even a Pollyanna, which is contrary to the spirit intended in the book *Pollyanna* by Eleanor H. Porter, on which the term is based. In the book, Pollyanna is not naïve nor oblivious to danger, but she does choose to look at the bright side of every situation even when it's sometimes tough to do so.

So what's wrong with rose-colored glasses? If we're coloring our lives happy, then we should all keep a pair handy! What's wrong with being optimistic, with seeing the good in others, and being able to visualize a good outcome? If we think about it, we realize there's not much benefit in taking a negative view, which is also known as *worrying*. We'd realize that we stand to gain more by looking for the best in any situation or thinking ahead to a better time.

This reminds me of a story about a man who broke his leg and ended up in the hospital. Convinced he was the victim of bad luck, he was miserable. But one of his nurses was a wonderful woman. They fell in love and later married. This convinced him that breaking his leg had actually been good luck because it enabled him to meet his wife.

You can look at almost every situation in at least two ways. It's better to find a way to view even bad situations in the most positive way you can muster, not because it will change the situation or outcome, but because *it will change your attitude* and increase your chances of survival and triumph.

Viktor Frankl (2006), one of the world's best-known Holocaust survivors, though facing daily horrors, began to see beyond the reality and discovered that everything could be taken away from us except our freedom to hope.

After suffering in four concentration camps, including Auschwitz, from 1942 to 1945, Frankl was released. His wife, parents, and family had all died in the camps. Frankl went on to become a psychotherapist and developed a treatment called logotherapy, which theorized that our primary motivation for living is our search for meaning in life. He believed that if we can find personal meaning in life, then we can overcome dismal circumstances.

Frankl's experiences in the concentration camps did not make him set on revenge or become insensitive or uncaring toward others' sufferings. Instead, he realized that the guards could take everything from him, including his life, but they couldn't take away his inner spirit, his search for meaning in life.

He believed there are three ways to discover meaning in your life: creating a work or doing a deed, experiencing something or encountering someone, and having the right attitude toward unavoidable suffering.

Frankl believed we can find meaning in life even when we are confronted by a hopeless situation, such as what he faced in the concentration camps. Throughout his life, until his death at age ninety-two, he lived what he believed. He had been a witness to and a participant in the discovery of man's amazing ability to defy and brave the worst conditions we can conceive.

To my knowledge, Frankl never said anything about wearing rose-colored glasses. That's my way of saying you should view your current situation as the path you are navigating in your search for your life's meaning.

Though Frankl was never given credit, Gore (2010) perceptively believed it was Frankl's views that laid the groundwork for positive psychology.

You are not alone

Everyone wants to be happy, but too many people are afraid that being happy will take too much time or will require something extreme on their part, like climbing

Mt. Everest or moving to another part of the world or giving up something of value.

Is such a fear holding you back from seeking your happiness?

If so, then I have great news for you. Even though happiness is being studied by academics and scientists and has become the latest trend, it is not reserved for the few. *Happiness is available to all of us!*

You don't need to make huge changes in your life to be happy, although positive changes will likely come about as a result of the small efforts you take to get started. It's like beginning to change your eating habits by reducing what you eat by just a little bit. It's important your early efforts toward change are easy so you won't get discouraged and can master them before moving to the next level.

Don't be intimidated by others you think are happier (or more fit) than you. They may not be. Maybe they have to put out a lot of effort to maintain their happiness, just as a bodybuilder must maintain a certain lifestyle in order to keep up that chiseled appearance.

I imagine how you must feel, though, since I've felt intimidated more than once as I was writing this book. After all, with so many great books on happiness out there, what could I add? Besides, I worried that my personal experiences wouldn't be dramatic enough, unique enough, or interesting enough to hold anyone's attention for very long.

I also know—and admit—that I'm not perfect or even

perfectly happy all the time. So who am I to write a book about happiness? I had to face these feelings throughout the writing process.

And yet I knew I had to write this book. I knew someone would benefit from what I have to say. No other writer, no matter how skilled, could tell *my* story. Only *I* could tell my story.

Likewise, *only you can be you*. Only *you* can tell your story. Only *you* can carry out your dream, whatever it may be. Only *you* can live your life.

> *You are successful the moment you start moving toward a worthwhile goal.*
>
> —Chuck Carlson

Happiness doesn't require complex skills

You don't have to understand the inner workings of happiness in order to attain it for yourself.

Do you hesitate to turn on the light switch because you don't understand how electricity works? Of course not. So don't think you have to understand everything about being happy in order to enjoy it for yourself.

We depend on modern conveniences, even though we don't understand how—or why—they work. In fact, we use our cell phones and computers and drive our cars with little concern for the internal processes taking place. As long as they work, we're thrilled.

Happiness is much like that.

You can, of course, benefit from learning about brain research, if you wish to study it, to understand better how the mind works. Or, if you wish, you can choose to study meditation in an Indian ashram. Or you can certainly delve into studying the physical and mental effects of exercise and diet. But the key is this: *You do not have to know anything new for the concepts in this book to work for you.*

This reminds me of the old joke about the man who goes to the doctor complaining, "Doc, my arm hurts when I do this," and he demonstrates by raising his arm in the air. And the doctor responds, "Then don't do that."

Sometimes the solution is as simple as to stop doing a small thing that causes you pain or hurt and substitute things that give you joy.

Everything you need to be happier is already dwells inside you.

You don't need to be perfect or wait until you make certain changes. The trait that you consider your greatest flaw may actually be your greatest asset. Some people think they'd be happier after they undergo cosmetic surgery to change their faces, teeth, or bodies. Hollywood and the world of high fashion have helped perpetuate the stress on physical perfection.

Lauren Hutton, famous model from the '70s and well known for her *Vogue* covers and for being "the face of Revlon," refused to have the gap in her teeth fixed. That gap became her signature. Fred Astaire, film star, singer, and one of the greatest dancers of all time, once said that if you make the same mistake enough times, it becomes your style. Just as a flaw can become an asset, Astaire's dance "mistakes" became the signature style for which he is still remembered. An aspiring actress might consider a high nasal twang with a Queens accent a flaw. But for popular film and TV actress Fran Drescher, it is this very endearing feature that has marked and boosted her career.

I poked fun at my husband's flaws (and mine) in this poem I wrote in 1972.

He Is No Romeo

Flora Morris Brown

Where is my Romeo?
Sir Lancelot or Galahad?
Where is the prince I thought I'd wed,
The charming Sheik of Bagdad?
Who is this Herbert who shares my bed?
He carries no sword nor rapier.
The only dragon he's ever slain
Had been buzzing about his ear.
My Herbert has no golden locks,
No Atlas' physique has he.
He's protruding here and receding there
And short where long should be.
My darling spouse is no Romeo,
No Casanova, and yet
We are quite well-suited,
'Cause I am no Juliet!

DISCONTENT CAN BE YOUR SAVIOR

The moment you realize you're not satisfied with a situation, person, job, location, or even yourself, your mind gets to work—processing ways to get out, over, or around it. If you don't heed the solutions that bubble to the surface, then your discontent will only grow.

Left to fester, your discontent can lodge itself in your body and mind with the potential to move from sadness to hopelessness and even physical illness. All of us experience some sadness, but when sadness persists, it can become depression, which is a chronic medical condition that most people do not just snap out of without help. Depression brings on physical and chemical changes in the body, causing sufferers to lose interest in life. Depression makes it difficult to manage daily tasks. If this sounds like you or someone you love, seek professional help immediately.

If you have a friend or loved one who is suffering from prolonged sadness or has been a victim of trauma, please resist the urge to comfort them by saying any of the following useless sentences:

I know how you feel.

Stop feeling sorry for yourself.

Snap out of it.

It's God's will.

Maybe God is punishing you.

Don't worry; the sun will come out tomorrow.

There's always someone worse off than you.

Well-meaning though these clichés are, they can be more harmful than comforting. The best comfort you can offer is listening and being present. When appropriate, encourage simple actions, such as completing one small manageable task each day or getting out into the sunshine and moving the body by walking. In addition to seeking professional help, your friend or loved one could consider joining a support group. Begin the search for support groups at http://www.mentalhealthamerica.net.

If you let your discontent spur you to positive action, it becomes your savior. You will no longer need advice or permission to do everything. You will no longer wonder whether the thing you need to do is the right thing to do. You will just know it's time and it's the right thing to do. You will know, at the deepest level, what you need to do. And you will know you will be okay.

You may decide to act quickly—just as you would jump to safety out of the path of an oncoming truck. Or you may decide to act carefully and deliberately, as if neatly packing for a very long trip. There is no right or wrong way to act when you make this change. As long as your actions for change are positive, do no harm to others, and are in harmony with the universe, then your success is assured.

In your search for happiness, look inside yourself. Here are some ways to start:

1. *Get quiet.* It doesn't matter whether you choose meditation, yoga, prayer, or just sit still. Choose what feels comfortable and natural for you.
2. *Try to remember some meaningful activities or accomplishments in your life and then focus on things you really enjoyed doing.* Maybe it was building model cars, making a surfboard, speaking to your son's Boy Scout troop, or trying new recipes. It doesn't matter what it was. Only you know what made you feel good about yourself and gave you joy—not only while you were doing them, but even now as you remember them. They may be things you haven't done since childhood or youth. Write down as many as you can.
3. *Make a plan to do at least one of these things as soon as possible.* Plan it, put it on your calendar, treat it with the same importance as you would any other appointment. Don't let anyone talk you out of it. And don't stand yourself up for this appointment.
4. *Before the event, think about how much fun you'll have.* Visualize yourself smiling, laughing, and enjoying the event.
5. *After the event, share with a friend how much fun you had.* Describe the activity in full.
6. *Savor the memory.* Take pictures or journal about the event.
7. *Repeat the process with another activity. Select another activity you listed in #2 and follow the process again.*

At this point, I must issue another warning

Don't postpone doing what you enjoy in hopes of finding someone to participate with you. If you can't locate companions who share your interests, then go alone. Depending on the activity, you may find others already there who are alone, too.

Before I discovered a theater-going group, for example, if I couldn't find a companion, I attended the theater alone. During intermission, I'd always find someone to chat with before we scurried back to our seats. I go to the movies alone if I can't find a friend or relative to join me. Why should I miss a movie because it's not convenient or interesting to someone else?

When I decided to tour Italy, I signed up with a tour group. I had never used this tour service, but the timing and price were right, so I flew to Rome alone and met up with the group there. Three ladies were also traveling alone in the group of forty. We became good companions and everyone had a great time.

Once you set out to be happy, only you can decide what your personal happiness will look like.

Happiness is a choice

As we've seen, research and discussions about happiness attribute a portion of our happiness to genetics and upbringing, but a large portion of our happiness comes from the choices we make.

By happiness, I don't, of course, mean a constant

state of elation or giddiness, but a state of contentment that comes from living in a way that gives us and others pleasure and enables us to recover from pain. Many of us never get to this state because we spend too much time doing things that don't give us pleasure—things we feel obligated to do or things others insist we do.

No matter how much advice there is about how to be happy, and it seems to multiply daily, ultimately only you can know what makes you happy. My youngest daughter and I love to travel, but we have very different ideas about how to do it. She likes to explore on her own, investigating sites as they appear. I like guided tours so I can see as much as possible in a day.

When we went to Europe, we were quite a pair. She had her *Let's Go Europe* written by Harvard students; I was clutching my copy of *Europe Through the Back Door* by Rick Steves (https://www.ricksteves.com/), the travel writer and TV host who offers more than twenty-five years of budget travel advice. In Paris, my daughter wanted to go on a walking tour of one of the famous gardens, then seek out a food stand on a back street where her guidebook promised delicious food. I wanted to go to the Louvre and then sit at one of the outdoor cafes sipping overpriced cappuccino while doing some people watching. I wanted to catch a cab to the Eiffel Tower, but her book said it was too crowded and we could get great shots of the famous tower from the balcony of La Samaritaine, one of Paris's largest department stores (which has since been closed). We did get some great photos. But I didn't make it to the Eiffel Tower on that trip.

However, in London, I insisted on going to 221B Baker Street, where according to the stories written by Sir Arthur Conan Doyle, Sherlock Holmes lived between 1881 and 1904. Even though Holmes is a fictional character, his address is so famous that it is protected by the British government today as it was in Victorian times. Although my daughter didn't share my fascination and determination to visit Holmes, we compromised, and away we went, walking the 1.8 miles from the British Museum to visit the digs of Sherlock Holmes.

I'm all for expanding my comfort zone, and sometimes I do venture out to share some of her interests. After all, I stayed in several hostels during our trip after she agreed that we'd stay in a hotel in Paris first. My point is that if you ask people what makes them happy, the answers will be different every time, but the result will always be the same. Each of us has our own personal definition of happiness.

I encourage anyone seeking happiness and fulfillment to explore the many opportunities that abound, but you must eventually pick what resonates with you. What makes your heart sing? Wayne Dyer is frequently quoted as having said, "When you change the way you look at things, the things you look at change."

One day I noticed a clerk at my local store had lost a lot of weight. I complimented her and asked how she'd done it. "I just ate sensibly," she shared. "Diets just don't work for me."

The problem with the word "diet" is it has the word "die" in it! If we can think of the way we eat as an "eating plan," then we're already on a positive road to success. The clerk's "eating plan" worked for her because it was of her own making and allowed for flexibility and variation.

Many of the popular celebrity, fad, and medical diets don't work because they are imposed from the outside. Most people who succeed in losing weight do it slowly and sensibly by changing their eating and living habits.

In our search for happiness, many of us look outside ourselves. We buy more gadgets, clothes, shoes, and equipment. We work harder and longer hours to make more money. Now don't get me wrong—I love those things, too. But the newness eventually wears off and we grow tired from working too much. Then we're overcome by feelings of emptiness or discontent. That's because *things* don't fill or fulfill us. What fulfills us over time is participating in meaningful activities, being with those we care about who share our interests and, most of all, learning to accept and love ourselves just as we are.

Thinking about change is the first step

Are you thinking about making a change in your life?

Sure you are. That's why you're reading this book. Congratulations! You've already taken the first step.

Without any conscious action beyond buying and opening this book, you have begun to shift from something that isn't pleasing you to finding your happiness—just by recognizing that you want to make a change.

MAYBE YOU SHOULD DISREGARD SENSIBLE ADVICE

A slow death comes for those who don't revolt when they're unhappy in their work or in love. Who don't risk the certain for the uncertain in order to follow a dream. Who don't allow themselves, at least once in their life, to disregard sensible advice.

—Pablo Neruda

Following a dream may be difficult to do. Most of us were raised to take sensible advice, as in "Finish your dinner…," "Get a good job…," "Don't talk to strangers…," "Be satisfied with what you've got or done...," and "Don't travel abroad, it's not safe."

While good advice is usually well-intentioned,

following it does not always lead to personal happiness. For example:

- Finishing your dinner can lead to overeating, heartburn, and obesity.
- Getting a good job might lead to more boredom and stress than happiness.
- As for strangers, isn't everyone other than your family a stranger until you meet them?
- Being satisfied brings an abrupt halt to innovation and invention.
- It's not safe to get on the freeway, either. However, you must do it to get to where you're going.

When your heart and mind are longing to go in a new direction, you must disregard some of that sensible advice. *Not* doing what you love is what you will later regret more than anything else.

> *Twenty years from now you will be more disappointed by the things that you didn't do than by the ones you did. So throw off the bowlines. Sail away from the safe harbor. Catch the trade winds in your sails. Explore. Dream. Discover.*
>
> —Attributed to that well-known pessimist Mark Twain

There are two sides to getting what you want

A frequent theme of the classic TV show *The Twilight Zone* was getting what you want and then discovering that you didn't want everything that went with it. In a third-season episode, "The Trade-Ins," an aging couple, John and Marie Holt, visit a company that offers youthful bodies to those who are aging. The Holts love each other very much and look forward to reliving their youth together. They browse the showcases that display young couples in happy positions, select the bodies they want, and place their order. Then they learn they have only enough money for one body. Because John is suffering more physical pain, they decide he should get the transforming operation.

After his transformation is complete, however, they catch a glimpse of themselves in a mirror. John realizes the absurdity of it. He's in a youthful body, but Marie is still trapped in her aging body.

In the last scene, the couple is holding hands and walking away from the camera. John has returned to his old body, and he and Marie will undoubtedly spend their remaining years aging together.

Here's another example. My daughter and I joined some friends one Easter week to visit another friend who had moved to El Salvador seven years earlier. This friend had fallen in love with the country and its people. He often invited us to visit him. After I retired, I finally made the trip.

I spent hours sitting on his patio or lying in his hammock, gazing out at the ocean just beyond the pool.

I took in the beautiful vista as I listened to tropical music playing on the boom box in the background. It was a setting most of us imagine when we visualize paradise.

Before you invest any time being envious, however, be aware: Paradise has a downside.

I discovered that while I love looking out at the ocean waves, I do not love walking in the sand. Once I'd walked in the sand, I just couldn't get it out of my shoes! And walking barefoot was out of the question—in the daytime, the sand was just too hot for my footsies.

I also learned that insects love paradise, too. Those El Salvadoran mosquitoes made a tasty feast of this newcomer. They found all the repellent I lathered on very tasty. Then there were the tiny brown ants. What were they doing in the kitchen?

I came to enjoy the early morning, just after a shower, best. For those few minutes, I felt refreshed and clean. But soon I was dripping wet, as sweat poured down my face and moistened my hair. It's tough to look sexy and wipe sweat off your face at the same time!

What I enjoyed most about the trip were the Salvadoran people. I felt safe everywhere we went. Despite my tentative Spanish, we easily shopped, dined, and visited new friends. Our host introduced us to a number of his Salvadoran friends, and we participated in Good Friday activities there.

But as the old-timers say, "Paradise ain't all it's cracked up to be."

I encourage you to visit your own paradise—wherever you may find it. But just remember that close up, there's more than one side to paradise. You might even find some bugs! The sooner you accept and feel content with this idea, the happier you'll be. You can't have one side of paradise without the other.

Are you stuck in preparation mode?

A popular inspirational speaker once commented to her audience that she recognized a number of them from previous seminars. Although she was glad to have their support, she cautioned them not to get stuck in continuing to take seminars, but to get busy putting into practice what they had learned.

Many students take classes and pursue degrees, always preparing to live life *later*, after they finish this class or that seminar and earn another degree. I'm guilty of taking webinar after webinar in search of more knowledge and one more skill. It's a delaying tactic. It signals procrastination, lack of confidence, and fear.

Unlike school, in life the test comes first, then the lesson. Get busy living and learn as you go.

It's like believing you need to thoroughly read the manual to your new computer or digital camera before you can start to use it. Just the opposite is true. You can only learn to use something by trying it out and making mistakes, then finding solutions on your own. No manual can cover every contingency. Young people subscribe to the theory that technology should be easy enough to understand without a manual. I think this is the basis of the term *user-friendly*.

By the time we finally understand that it's okay to live without "reading the manual," many of us have wasted our young years in a never-ending state of preparation. We took those classes and attended those seminars, but we never really lived. Sadly, some of us make it to adulthood without having left the starting gate. Some suffer pangs of regret and even die with a book, song, or dream still inside them.

Don't let that be you.

When Rubin (2009), lawyer, blogger, and author, decided that she could probably be happier, she set out on a yearlong project. Her goal was to try out changes in her personal and work life, then chronicle her results and insights on her blog, *The Happiness Project*. The result was her *New York Times* #1 bestselling book, *The Happiness Project: Or, Why I Spent a Year Trying to Sing in the Morning, Clean My Closets, Fight Right, Read Aristotle, and Generally Have More Fun*. She not only examined her beliefs, habits, and lifestyle but also shared what she gleaned from the happiness research and advice from many of the other happiness books.

Preparing for happiness requires examining your beliefs

While you may not want to share your efforts at happiness with the world like Rubin did, examining your beliefs will be the first step in preparing to increase your happiness.

Our beliefs determine how we filter new information, gain knowledge, and make choices that direct our lives. They are the blueprints for our lives and guide our habits, actions, and reactions. Mostly we live by unexamined, hand-me-down beliefs from our parents and society. If, for example, our parents believed that we were strong and capable, then we will approach disappointments in life with determination and a positive plan of action. If, on the other hand, we were raised to believe that the world is a scary place and we are not safe, we may always believe that disappointments are inevitable and that we don't have much power or choice in how our lives will go. In this case, we may follow what others tell us to do without thinking about it ourselves.

Our thoughts based on our beliefs either aid us in taking positive action toward our success and happiness or limit and block us from moving toward our goals. They often lead to self-sabotage. If I believe I'm a worthwhile person who deserves good treatment, I'm less likely to fall victim to domestic violence. If I believe I'm unworthy of good treatment, I will think I deserve to be a victim of abuse and have trouble breaking away from it.

Byron Katie (http://thework.com & Katie, 2003), speaker, spiritual transformer, and author, advocates that we not just discover our beliefs but also question them. She came to this understanding in 1986 after she woke up on the floor of a halfway house after having suffered ten years of depression, rage, and self-loathing. That morning, she suddenly realized that when she believed her stressful thoughts, she suffered. When she questioned them, she no longer suffered. This epiphany turned her life around and launched her career of helping others through her self-inquiry method.

Before her lapse into depression, Katie is said to have lived an ordinary life. She had been through two marriages and had three children and a successful career. In the grips of depression, she seldom left her house, and her children tiptoed past her door to avoid triggering one of her rages. Even in the halfway house she eventually checked herself into, she was placed alone in an attic room because the other residents were afraid of her.

Friends and family must have been skeptical that Katie's sudden emergence from depression was permanent. Once they all realized that the old Katie was not coming back, however, they wanted to know how she did it. Since 1993, she has been on the road sharing her technique, writing books, making TV appearances, and running retreats and workshops.

Her method is simple and profound and is based on asking yourself four questions about whatever is troubling you. Learn about her process at http://thework.com

When my oldest daughter moved away from Southern California to make her own life in the Bay Area, I was delighted to witness her independence and resourcefulness as she landed a job, found a wonderful apartment, and made new friends. She was finally following her dream.

In our family, we always lived within a few miles

of each other, even after starting our families. After she moved more than six hundred miles away, my daughter and I talked on the phone almost every day, I spent either Thanksgiving or her birthday visiting her and enjoying the sights of her new home. After a few years, however, she announced that she didn't want to celebrate her upcoming birthday. It would be her forty-second. I was calling to suggest a play I thought we'd both enjoy. I was taken aback. What had brought this on? Was she depressed? As a mom, wasn't there something I needed to *do*?

Her frequent calls home became less frequent or were replaced by very short emails. "I'm fine." She assured me she was okay and asked me to respect her wishes to "find herself." But I didn't know she was lost. I was distraught, not with any specific worry, but a flood of what-ifs. She still acknowledged my birthday and Christmas, but I felt a gap. Part of me was panicky and wanted to show up at her house unannounced to find out what was wrong. Trusted friends, a therapist, and prayer advised me against doing that.

Instead, I bought Katie's book, *Loving What Is* (Katie, 2003), based on the same four questions as The Work (http://thework.com). Each question had subquestions that encourage deeper questioning. By working through the questions, especially the fourth one, I was able to get relief from worry about my daughter's well-being and restore my peace of mind. I learned to love the relationship my daughter and I now have. As Katie pointed out, when we're feeling stress, it's because we are not accepting that what is, is.

Four years after the shift in our relationship, my oldest daughter and I talk more frequently. She has a significant other and enjoys her life and manages quite well without me. She drove down to visit on Mother's Day. After accepting that what is, is, I'm enjoying our new relationship.

Many people find comfort in the body of beliefs that make up a religion or spiritual belief system. Some perfectly wonderful people do not believe in God or any Higher Power. Others have a strong belief in God or a Higher Power, but believe they are being directed to kill everyone who does not share their beliefs. Most of us are somewhere in between. We believe in versions of God or a Higher Power and consult with them, rely upon them, and acknowledge or call upon them to help us lead better lives.

When you discover the beliefs that are guiding your life, you'll be ready to move toward your goals and achieve happiness.

Spiritual Beliefs Are for Daily Living, Not Just for Weekly Worship Services

Increasingly, people around the world are describing themselves as spiritual rather than religious, disassociating from church-going as an indicator of faith. In my view, spiritual beliefs are broader than religion and should drive your daily life.

My friend Jim Holley was an example of someone who lived by his spiritual beliefs. He and his family were members of a church I attended in Los Angeles. We taught Sunday school together. His wife and kids and I sang in the choir. I was still single and in college when we first met, and I even babysat their kids a few times. When I got married, our families enjoyed many happy visits, and our children (though his were older than mine) participated in some of the same activities. Jim became our insurance representative and gave me lots of good advice that serves me well to this day.

As a loving and caring friend, he called periodically to check up on me. During the years when my kids were young and I was attending graduate school, I sometimes answered the phone in a foul mood. I had retired from teaching to return to school full time, and my husband and I decided it was also a good time to have our third child. There were days when things would be clipping along just fine until a broken water heater or leaking fuel pump took a deep bite out of our already strained budget and altered my mood. So when Jim asked how I was doing, there were times when I growled and told him about the latest calamity.

But he never let me wallow in the pity party I was trying to host. Without breaking stride, he always had me open my Bible to a certain verse. The specific verse depended on the situation or the level of my growling. Then he insisted I read it aloud to him. That always helped me.

Jim passed away many years ago, but his support, encouragement, and words of comfort live on. Any time I feel stressed, I can snap back by repeating one of Jim's favorite verses: "This is the day which the Lord has made: let us rejoice and be glad in it" (Psalm 118:24 NASB).

Now I pass this verse along to you to repeat any time the world threatens to overtake you. I hope it will lighten your load and lift your mood.

But while we are eager to make changes in our lives, it is a mistake to think we can change everything. We still have to accept that there are some things we can't change.

Happiness researchers agree that we come into this world with a genetic makeup that accounts for about half of who we are. About one tenth of who we are is determined by our upbringing, economic level, education level, and other environmental factors. We can change the remaining 40 percent to suit ourselves.

Seligman (2007) pointed out that we just can't change some things, including sexual identity and sexual orientation. Seligman doesn't believe gaining insight into our childhoods is very helpful. Instead, he believes that by conscious thinking, we can learn optimism, control our moods, unlearn panic, and cure depression.

Fortunately, feeling better about ourselves, choosing pleasing experiences, and taking a positive outlook are all generally within our control. And the good news is that these changes take place internally with no monetary cost. Some people, however, don't get this. They concentrate on external changes and, unfortunately, miss the mark entirely. *Change must come from within.*

In this age of self-improvement, it's common to hear about people who subject themselves to one cosmetic surgery after another in an attempt to enhance, reshape, or diminish parts of their bodies. Even if they are fortunate enough to have successful surgeries, they still are powerless to control the changes to their "modifications" that come with natural aging. That's when, despite the surgeries, and if the self-esteem issues that caused them to believe they needed surgery to be accepted or loved are still intact, they discover that happiness still eludes them.

I'd like to add to Dr. Seligman's list of things we can't change. The biggest thing we can't change is *other people*. Once we accept that, and instead look inward to the things we can change about ourselves, then we are on the road to finding the happiness we seek.

> Color your life *exciting* by using red to draw attention. Red is the color of movement and energy, so don't use it on the baby's nursery walls. It's the most dynamic of all colors, but overusing it can cause restlessness.

Summary

Learn to be a positive thinker—even when everything around you seems negative, remember that your happiness is up to you. No one else can do it for you.

Don't be eager to abandon what you think are your flaws. They may turn out to be your greatest assets.

Congratulate yourself for even thinking about change. You have taken the first step.

You don't always have to take sensible advice. Evaluate what you hear or learn and decide what's best for you. Be willing to color outside the lines.

Be ready to accept the good and bad that come with getting what you want.

Get out of preparation mode. You're ready! Stop thinking you are helpless and start helping yourself.

Question your troubling beliefs. Turn them around to get to the truth on the other side.

Practice your spiritual beliefs daily. Accept that there are some things you can change… and some you can't.

Happiness Flashback

I took lots of photos of my children to chronicle major and minor events in their lives. They were so used to posing for pictures during their activities that, no matter how upset or tearful they were, when I pulled out a camera, they froze in place and broke into smiles. Then they returned to whatever dispute or turmoil they had been involved in at the time. It wasn't until recently that I realized my insistence that they smile on cue was exactly what my mother did.

EMBRACING HAPPINESS

Unhappiness is not knowing what we want and killing ourselves to get it

—Don Herold

When I was a child in St. Louis, Missouri, black families focused on the essentials: shelter, food, clothes, church. We were raised to steer clear of behavior that could land us or our family in trouble with the law or with white people… which was the same thing.

Growing up in a segregated neighborhood had its comforts, though. Everything we needed was nearby. My elementary school was two blocks away, my church one block from my elementary school, and my high school was just an eight-block walk. The Jewish storekeepers and movie theater owners were friendly and mostly patient with us kids scampering through their pricey inventories. After all, we were the reason they were profitable.

We kids were encouraged by our teachers and church leaders to achieve an education and better life. After all, they were victims of segregation, too. Even the neighborhood drunkard leaning against a power pole shouted out words of encouragement as he saw us strolling by on our way to school or church.

There were a few bullies, of course, who tested their power over us, but my youngest sister, Mildred, although two years younger than I, called their bluffs early. I soon had an invisible wall of protection around me. "Don't bother her," the other kids said. "That's Mildred's sister."

Happiness—at least not genuine happiness—is a luxury oppressed people often think they can't afford. After all, how can you be really happy when you can't even go to certain movie theaters or public venues because you had the poor judgment to be born black? Anyone running around saying they were happy was judged with a suspicious eye. Clearly, that black child must be shallow, addle-brained, or silly.

And yet my mother always strove for a better life for us. Because she was an excellent seamstress, for example, she made us stylish wool jumpers and pleated skirts for school. She created full-length, formal dresses for our concert performances in the Children's Choir at church. She sewed us unique Halloween costumes. My favorite costume was a gypsy skirt she made for me, sewing together wide strips cut from an old white sheet that she had painstakingly dyed different colors.

Mom was never willing to settle for the cheaper

toys that were easily accessible at the local stores. She listened to Art Linkletter's *House Party* radio show while she was working on customers in her beauty shop and made mental notes on which toys were recommended for their entertainment and educational value. Then, months before Christmas shopping officially started, she put our toys on layaway at the big downtown St. Louis department stores. Every Tuesday on her day off, she caught the bus and went downtown to shop and make another payment on our toys. Until I wrote this, I never thought about how she got our toys home. We didn't own a car.

Negro spirituals left over from the days of slavery, like "I Got Shoes," promised delayed happiness: "When I get to Heaven, gonna put on my shoes and shout all over God's Heaven." But my mother embraced the possibility of happiness for us in the here and now, and worked at arranging for as much happiness as possible for her family, sometimes against some pretty tough odds.

Bring happiness into the present

We often talk about happiness as though it's lurking "out there," somewhere outside ourselves. We see evidence of happiness in other people, but we aren't sure we can experience it ourselves. The truth is that *you can't be happy in the future unless you're happy now*. The potential for happiness is already inside you, just as the potential for a plant is already there inside a seed.

This brings to mind an experience I had after I

retired. I decided to plant a vegetable garden. I was intrigued not just with the idea of eating healthier meals, but also with the chance to watch nature close-up and in action. So I bought a variety of herb and vegetable seeds from my local garden shop and planted them alongside my house. Within just a few days of watering, I could see tiny green signs of life peeking up through the dirt.

I love zucchini, so I'd purchased two little potted plants. As they grew and became recognizable, I saw that, sure enough, one of them was forming the familiar green squash shape. But the other one was yellow and had a bulging bottom. I reread the identification cards that came with both little pots. Sure enough, they were identical: "Squash, Zucchini."

Soon it became clear that something was wrong. No matter what the label said, one of the plants wasn't the zucchini I thought I'd bought. It was obvious one had been mislabeled. Even though the yellow squash had been labeled zucchini, with my care and nurturing, it produced what it had inside all along: the potential to become a yellow squash.

Like that plant, no matter what labels get attached to us, we have the potential to manifest our own happiness. Once we recognize the "seed of happiness" within us right now, we can free ourselves to grow and bring it forth.

Just as my zucchini plant yielded zucchini while the yellow squash plant yielded yellow squash, your happiness is not the same as another person's happiness. I don't imagine either plant (if plants can think) wished it was the same as the other one. Each squash just grew into what it was meant to be.

ALLOW YOURSELF TO BE HAPPY

Don't rely on someone else for your
happiness and self-worth. Only you can be
responsible for that. If you can't love and
respect yourself, no one else
will be able to make that happen. Accept who
you are—completely;
the good and the bad, and make changes as
YOU see fit—not
because you think someone else wants you to
be different.

—Stacey Charter

If you've been unhappy most of your life, you may be astonished to learn that you have the power to change your attitude. If you're a hardcore pessimist, you may even derive some pleasure from being negative, even though it eventually makes you sad. Pessimism may even lead to depression. (If you're mostly cynical and enjoy it, embrace it. I think we're in danger of becoming cynical as we get older.)

Listening to other people gripe and complain, we hear how much we restrict our own happiness by focusing on the negative. For example, one day I listened to a friend share a string of problems in her life. Suddenly it occurred to me that none of the things she saw as problems were really that serious, so I asked her to tell me about the *good* things going on in her life. She was taken aback.

"What do you mean?" she asked.

"Well, let me help you get started," I said. "You have a loving husband, you're doing the work you love, you live in a beautiful home, you can afford to travel wherever you want, and you have raised two successful children."

"You're right," she said. "I must remember the good."

Not only do we get caught up in recounting our "problems," but I think we actually enjoy sharing the negative more than rejoicing in the positive.

Where does this come from, and how do we learn to embrace happiness? Perhaps some of us think that dwelling on happy thoughts will jinx us. Because my husband and I separated right after Christmas one year, for example, one relative thought I had jinxed our family and brought on this marital split because I had been writing about positive things in our family every year in my Christmas letters.

Many of us don't enjoy happiness because we have an aversion to it. Many of us were brought up to mistrust happiness and to avoid embracing it for fear it won't last. Sadly, this leaves us more comfortable with misery than with joy in our lives.

To enjoy happiness, we must allow it into our lives.

Align your life with happiness

Years ago, my husband, our four children, and I returned from a vacation in Yosemite National Park, a spectacularly beautiful wilderness park in the Sierra Nevada Mountains of California. I shared the highlights of our vacation with one of my friends—the trip by car, our stay in a tent cabin (a cabin with solid walls, but a canvas roof and door flaps), horseback riding, and cooking around the campfire. My friend was absolutely fascinated. She was also puzzled as to how we were able to plan such a vacation.

"How did you know about Yosemite and how to get there?" she asked me.

I was a little confused by her question. "What do you mean?"

"How did you figure out how to get there?"

"Oh," I responded, "I got a map from the Automobile Club of America. They marked the route for us. There was information about accommodations on the back of the map. I just called to make reservations."

Even though that was in the days before the Internet, there were many resources for planning vacations.

Just as my friend was puzzled about how to plan a vacation and how to get where you're going, some people are puzzled about how to set up their lives. If you desire happiness, then you must plan and organize your life in a way that will allow happiness. Here are some ways to do this.

1. *Spend time with people you enjoy.* You may think this is obvious, but we don't always practice it. My friend Connie (name changed) complained about her friend Shelly's (name changed) annoying habit of always being short of money when they went

out to lunch. But even though it bothered her, Connie just paid the check. Then she complained about her cheap friend Shelly.

When I asked why she continued to go to lunch with Shelly, she answered, "Because she's my friend."

Connie felt stuck. She didn't realize that no one else viewed Shelly as a friend. Worst of all, Connie didn't know that she had the power to change how and with whom she spent her time.

2. *Avoid toxic people and sad situations.* You don't have to look far to find people (maybe even some of your relatives) who enjoy complaining and griping about personal and world problems. Acknowledging what is going on in the news and fretting a bit are harmless. But constantly being exposed to people who revel in spewing vicious gossip, repeating the gory details of the latest mass murder, or retelling blow by blow the pain they suffered during their last surgery is exhausting. It's guaranteed to sour and pull down your mood.

   Keep your environment pleasing by not allowing toxic people to disturb the harmony and tranquility. Likewise, if horror movies make you upset, or loud music disturbs you, then don't go to those movies and stay away from places where loud music is playing. (Read more about identifying and avoiding toxic people in Chapter 7.)

3. *Take care of your spiritual and emotional needs.* Every one of us can benefit from taking a step back from our day-to-day life to get quiet, to reflect, and to calm our emotions. To neglect this is like trying to drive your car without giving it adequate maintenance. Eventually your car will break down from neglect.

   You need adequate renewal so you can have the energy and the strength of mind and emotions to handle the challenges of life as well as enjoy personal growth. When you don't make time to meet your spiritual and emotional needs, you set yourself up for burnout, exhaustion, apathy, and possibly depression.

Covey (2013) calls his Habit #7 "Sharpening the Saw." He tells a story about a man who was cutting firewood for his family. He was working and sweating and straining. An observer could see that this chore was really a big challenge and asked him if his saw was sharp. The man said that it sure didn't seem too sharp. The observer then recommended that he take a few moments and sharpen the saw. The man replied, "I am too busy sawing to take time to sharpen my saw."

Taking care of your spiritual and emotional needs is "sharpening your saw." It's renewing yourself. If you don't take time to renew yourself, you will be working harder than necessary just to get your needs met.

You can experience spiritual renewal without subscribing to any specific religious belief. Some of the ways are through meditation, reading motivational materials (books, poetry, quotations), listening to inspirational speakers, taking a nature walk, or enjoying beautiful music. (In Chapter 7, you will learn about additional ways to meet your spiritual needs.)

You can meet your emotional needs by forming meaningful relationships and associations with others. Whatever enables you to fortify your mind and spirit for dealing with the everyday will enable you not only to cope with life, but also to enjoy a happier life.

SHOW GRATITUDE FOR ALL THE GOOD IN YOUR LIFE

Emmons (2007) has conducted research on gratitude, its components, and its benefits. He admitted that when he began his research on gratitude, he didn't expect it to be as deep and complex as it turned out to be. Soon, however, he discovered that gratitude was one of the few things that could measurably change our lives.

He pointed out that being grateful includes acknowledging good and recognizing that it comes from outside ourselves. It doesn't matter whether the gift is material or nonmaterial. When we recognize the gift, thank the giver, or express thankfulness for the gift, we are transformed.

Emmons identified a number of benefits of gratitude and its connection to happiness. Three benefits are:

- Practicing gratitude can increase happiness levels by around 25 percent.
- Keeping a gratitude journal for as little as three weeks will improve your sleep and increase your energy.
- Increasing happiness by practicing gratitude will be sustained over a long period of time.

Adopt a winning attitude

How we think about the future is generally described in two ways. We are either optimists or pessimists. An optimist is often said to be someone who sees a glass as half full, whereas a pessimist is said to be someone who sees it as half empty.

Even though we've been told that optimists tend to be more successful, folks stuck in pessimism are hard-pressed to turn themselves around. Part of the reason is that pessimists are so accustomed to seeing the dark side that they've lost sight, if they ever had it, of the bright side.

My second daughter showed a pessimistic side at an early age. When she was in elementary school, she complained and worked herself into tears each time a new concept was introduced. "I can't do it," she wailed after she had mastered addition and the teacher was introducing subtraction. She repeated her doubts and fears when multiplication was introduced, and with division, too. When I reminded her of how she'd conquered new things in the past, she finally calmed down and learned each new concept.

When confronted with a problem or a challenge, we all tell ourselves a story. Optimists tell hopeful stories. They expect to succeed. Pessimists tell sad stories. They expect to fail.

Here are three descriptions of pessimists and optimists.

A pessimist is one who feels bad when he feels good for fear he'll feel worse when he feels better.

—Anonymous

The optimist sees the rose and not its thorns; the pessimist stares at the thorns, oblivious to the rose.

—Kahlil Gibran

Pessimist: One whom when he has the choice of two evils, chooses both.

—Oscar Wilde

Let something bad or challenging happen, and the pessimist immediately thinks of the worst-case scenario. This inevitably results in misery, but he repeats it over and over. The results are not only unhappiness, but in extreme cases, prolonged sadness.

Some pessimists, however, succeed despite their negativity. They know they're pessimists, and they're determined to overcome their negative outlook and expectations. They work to create success. They take an extreme view of optimism, so while they can't see themselves as optimists, they work to overcome their pessimism in order to succeed. They see an optimist as someone who skips through the meadows in the face of danger, oblivious to rocks, singing the song Bobby McFerrin made popular, "Don't Worry, Be Happy."

Does optimism have drawbacks?

Maintaining hope in the face of danger or bad news may not always be the best strategy. Norem (2002) believed that while optimism is great, some folks are prone to anticipating the worst. For these people, trying to put on a happy face doesn't work.

Because these "defensive pessimists," to use Norem's words, believe in Murphy's Law ("If something can go wrong, it will"), they quash their anxiety with careful planning and defensive strategies. When planning a dinner party, for example, a defensive pessimist considers all the disasters that could occur if certain people sat next to each other and reworks the seating chart and plans for new topics of conversation. An optimist, on the other hand, thinks of all this as unnecssary worry.

Like many of us, Norem viewed pessimists and optimists at extreme ends of a personality continuum. When I'm planning the seating for a dinner party, I don't see it as pessimistic to seat amiable folks next to each other. It just seems like wise planning to me!

Are there any benefits to being a pessimist?

In their research study, Gibson and Sanbonmatsu (2004) concluded that with gambling, pessimists tend to make safer choices than their optimistic counterparts. First they gave three groups of college students a list of questions to determine whether they were optimists or pessimists. Then they conducted three studies.

In the first study, the students were asked about their motivation to gamble and their feelings toward gambling after winning or losing. In the second study, students played several hands of blackjack with a ten-dollar reward they could either bet or keep. In the third study, participants played a simulated slot machine game to win chances at a $50 prize.

The researchers found that while the optimists tended to have a positive attitude, even toward their losses, they persisted in the face of losses, whereas the pessimists calculated their risks. Gibson and Sanbonmatsu interpreted this to mean that despite optimism's many benefits, there are common situations in which the pessimistic tendency to disengage is beneficial. In other words, they believed that optimists don't know when to quit or pull out of losing situations, such as a failing stock market or a failing entrepreneurial venture.

Coming to this conclusion, Gibson and Sanbonmatsu joined with many people who take the extreme view that optimism and pessimism are opposites and that we are either one or the other. They seem to believe that an optimist has the sense to duck when he sees a big rock coming toward his head. They seem to see a pessimist as someone who is *satisfied* with seeing the glass as half empty rather than someone who is working toward filling the glass.

I think the optimist believes that the world is mostly good and expects things to go well, but at the same time has the good judgment to evaluate situations to determine whether they are best for him. As I see it, the pessimist may believe that the world is mostly bad and expects things to go wrong, but she can still have the good judgment to evaluate a situation and participate in ventures that she believes will go well. Both optimists and pessimists can be healthy skeptics who withhold judgment on decisions until they check out the details.

While we may tend to be more of one than the other, no one is 100 percent optimistic or pessimistic. But those who lean toward optimism have the advantage of being able to cope with changes, overcome adversities, achieve their personal best, and create happiness for themselves.

Do you want to embrace happiness? In spite of what some see as the benefits of being pessimistic, countless studies have shown that an optimistic outlook enables us to live longer, be healthier, find positive solutions, look upon adversity as temporary, and persevere.

If you lean toward pessimism, there is good news for you. You can become more optimistic.

How?

By telling yourself a new story.

When a problem or challenge arises, it's important

to be aware of the story that pops into your head. Here's what they say:

> *Optimist: I'm quite capable. I can handle this. Let's see what I can do.*
>
> *Pessimist: I can't handle this. I'll fail. There's no point in even trying.*

If you're a pessimist, then flip the script! Talk back and talk louder than you did with the flawed script you've followed in the past. Challenge your old story with a new one.

> *Rescued pessimist: I can handle this. I've succeeded many times before. Now, where do I begin?*
>
> *Cowards die many times before their deaths; the valiant never taste of death but once.*
>
> —William Shakespeare, *Julius Caesar*

I ran across the following on a blog. It's an old story worth sharing:

> One day, a farmer's donkey fell down into a well. The animal cried piteously for hours as the farmer tried to figure out what to do. Finally, he decided the animal was old, and the well needed to be covered up anyway; it just wasn't worth it to retrieve the donkey. He invited all his neighbors

> to come over and help him, and they all grabbed shovels and began to shovel dirt into the well. At first, the donkey realized what was happening and cried horribly. Then, to everyone's amazement, he quieted down. A few shovel loads later, the farmer finally looked down the well. He was astonished at what he saw. With each shovel of dirt that hit his back, the donkey did something amazing. He shook it off into a little pile and took a step up to that new level. As the neighbors continued to shovel dirt on top of the animal, he shook it off and took another step up. Pretty soon, everyone was amazed to see the donkey step up over the edge of the well and happily trot off!
>
> The donkey had the right attitude about the dirt hitting his back. He didn't accept it as a death sentence. He shook off the dirt and took a step up.

Like the donkey in this story, at some point in our lives, we will find ourselves in deep trouble, distress, or what may seem like a hopeless situation. Our first reaction may be to cry and curse, lament our troubles, and fight against our situation. The sooner we turn from these fruitless reactions and calm ourselves, however, the sooner we can discover what positive actions we can take. We can shake off our troubles and rise to a satisfying solution. We cannot control or change others, but we can definitely control our reactions to outside circumstances.

Be a good landlord of your life

Renters love to complain about their landlords, who are portrayed as selfish, money-hungry, hard-hearted, negligent with repairs, and slow to make improvements. The landlord has been vilified throughout history as a mean and evil person worthy only of contempt.

If this is true, then why are you renting? Why not become your own property owner?

Save your excuses. I've heard them all.

Put yourself in the landlord's place for a moment. Would you be willing to risk your savings to buy income property, wade through the laws involved, rent the property to people like you, and then hope each month to receive your rent on time so you can pay your mortgage on time and more?

Perhaps you would. Perhaps you wouldn't.

Bear with me… I'm getting to the point.

The truth is that *you are a landlord*. You're the landlord of your own life, your body, your world. What kind of landlord are you?

Do you have a contract that outlines what you will do to maintain a good relationship with yourself? Do you have a life plan, written goals, and a life mission?

Do you maintain your life in a healthy and positive way? Do you properly water, feed, and cultivate your mind, body, and spirit?

Do you keep your word? Do you stick to your goals and make the best choices for yourself?

Do you pay the price required to keep your property

in good shape? Do you guard against pests and loiterers looking to make you their host?

As the landlord of your life, you have the responsibility—*the duty*—to create a happy life. No one knows exactly what the plan will be, only you. But there's no mistaking when your plan is in force. You feel good about the choices you make, even though they're not always perfect.

Even though you sometimes feel out of sorts or sad, you have a maintenance plan to take care of needed repairs. You spot leaks before they become costly holes. You use preventive measures to keep pests away before they become parasites.

You welcome only other caring and loving people to your "property;" people who honor and respect it as you do.

Be a good landlord to yourself. Take care of your life, and it will take care of you.

Take responsibility for your life

Seligman (2011) pointed out that we are born helpless and dependent on others to meet our needs and keep us alive. If all goes well, we depend less on others as we grow. We realize our own abilities and power to take care of our needs.

It's true that as we age, we may slip into a level of helplessness as our bodies, senses, and sometimes our minds betray us. However, there's a time between infancy and our last days that Seligman calls "unclaimed territory." During this in-between time, we're on our own. We choose how we will react to others, how events will shape our lives, and what direction we will take. What we think and do during this period largely determines our ability to embrace happiness.

Here are some things that you can think and do during this in-between time that will enable you to embrace happiness:

- Accept that you cannot control all the circumstances outside you.
- Take responsibility for controlling your reaction to those circumstances.
- Spend time with positive happy people.
- Avoid toxic people and sad situations.

Just as a single event is perceived differently by the optimist and the pessimist, so will the direction we take in our lives be determined by our perception.

When I took a photography class a few years ago, the teacher pointed out that a photo we see as black and white is also 18 percent gray. What we perceive as pure black or white really has many gradations. That idea stuck with me. I realized it's true about various aspects of life.

Life is not clear-cut or only black and white. There are many shades of gray, many answers to questions; there is no absolute right or wrong. No amount of preparation and goal setting will ensure that things go according to plan. Being able to accept uncertainty and go with occurrences we weren't expecting is an indicator of maturity and is essential for happiness.

> *Life is what happens to you while you're busy making other plans.*
>
> —John Lennon

Waiting for the perfect answer, the perfect mate, the absolutely right time will paralyze us. We can waste our entire lives just waiting. We have to make choices, but each choice requires some element of risk. Only those willing to risk will enjoy the rewards. Those who don't want to take a risk are not spared, though. Even inaction is a risk. Unfortunately, if you choose not to take a risk, the results probably won't be to your liking. Researchers say there are benefits and drawbacks of both optimism and pessimism. Ultimately, you must choose which suits you better. As an optimist, you may expect the best and have high hopes, but stick with a failing project longer than you should or be the victim of smooth-talking scam artists. As a pessimist, you may not expect things to turn out well. You will be right some of the time, thereby feeling gratified in your belief, but in the process neglect to celebrate when things go well.

No matter how much we plan and study, there will always be some uncertainty, pain, and disappointment in life. Get comfortable with this truth. It will help strengthen your confidence and belief in your ability to handle anything that comes up.

WHAT HAPPENS WHEN YOU DON'T GET WHAT YOU DON'T WANT?

I have worked all my adult life. In 1982, I grew weary of commuting seventy-two miles, roundtrip, to my university teaching job. I enjoyed my job, but then I received an opportunity to interview for a new one, which gave me the chance to cut my commute to only ten miles, which was exciting. Wearing my good blue "interview" suit, I showed up for the interview fairly confident that I would get the job. After all, my qualifications exceeded the minimum and I had always interviewed well.

But as the interview progressed, I felt the job slipping away. I was a bit taken aback, but I was right. A week after the interview, I received the obligatory "thank you for considering us" rejection letter.

Later as I reflected on this loss, I realized that I hadn't really wanted that job... at least not for the right reasons. It was a community college position, which in those days I considered a step back almost to high school teaching. And the school was located in a declining neighborhood. I had pushed all that aside with my eagerness to cut out the long commute so I could get back home to my family sooner every day.

That job was not to be. And now I'm very happy it didn't happen. I would have been miserable on that campus. I would likely have been looking for another job soon thereafter. Instead, I resigned from my university job to follow my dream to start a private tutoring program.

Have you ever gone after something you didn't really

want? Have you ever felt frustrated because you didn't know what you wanted? Maybe it's a blessing to not get what you didn't get.

Perhaps rejection is protection.

Spend some time reflecting on what you really want. It may not be the highest paying job or the shiniest object. It may be an experience or a destination that may not make sense to anyone else you know. That's not what matters at all.

What matters is that you spend this wonderful thing called your life going after what feels rewarding, uplifting, and fulfilling to you. In the end, that's all that matters.

Trying to avoid risk or randomness or only going after the sure thing leads some people to take shortcuts, some of which are dangerous and even illegal. Insider trading, quick college degrees, and embezzlement bring fast riches and achievement, but what is lost? Peace of mind and sometimes freedom.

Ultimately, it comes down to taking responsibility for your life. Once you've done this, then you are ready to embrace happiness. Reinhold Niebuhr, an American minister, ethicist, and political activist, composed a popular prayer. You'll recognize this excerpt, best known as the "Serenity Prayer," which is used in the Alcoholics Anonymous Recovery Program.

> *God, grant me the serenity to accept the things I cannot change, the courage to change the things I can, and the wisdom to know the difference.*

> Color your life *interesting* by taking stock of the colors in your wardrobe. Introduce a variety of colors to reflect your various moods.

SUMMARY

Embracing happiness means accepting yourself the way you are, allowing yourself to be happy, aligning yourself with happiness, and adopting a positive attitude.

Take responsibility for your happiness. While building relationships is part of it, don't count on others to define your self-worth. Spend time with people you enjoy, and avoid toxic people who enjoy creating negative situations and reactions.

Take care of your spiritual and emotional needs and keep your mind and spirit strong. Acknowledge those who have been good to you and have made a difference in your life. Gratitude is one of the easiest and quickest ways to sustain happiness.

Accept and become comfortable with the fact that life is filled with uncertainties.

Happiness doesn't require you to display a nonstop cheery disposition, but it does mean taking responsibility for your own life. As soon as you give up the notion of being perfect and are willing to risk going after what you want, then you have already opened your arms to embrace happiness.

Such as are your habitual thoughts; such also will be the character of your mind; for the soul is dyed by the color of your thoughts.

—Marcus Aurelius

Take the Happiness Pledge

Flora Morris Brown

Each day when I awake and discover I'm still alive,

I know I have another chance to grow, to learn, to thrive.

So as I enter the world anew, I will bypass the door marked CRAPPY

And with a smile on my face and a song in my heart,

Walk through the door marked HAPPY.

Happiness Flashback

I bought Christmas gifts and toys for my children all year round when things were on sale and available. Then I hid their toys in various places all over the house. One Christmas morning after the kids had opened their toys and were happily playing with them, I remembered I had neglected to put one toy under the tree.

Oh, no! The Cabbage Patch doll my youngest wanted so much was still in the far back of my closet. How was I going to handle this and maintain the Santa Claus myth?

While the kids were busy playing away from the tree, I quickly retrieved the Cabbage Patch doll from her hiding place and put her under the tree, then placed other boxes and packaging around her.

Then I called out to my youngest. "Did you get everything from under the tree?"

"Yes."

"There still seems to be something under the tree—over there in the back."

"No," she said impatiently. "I got everything,"

"Come and take another look."

"Okay." She was clearly annoyed. She walked toward the tree and reached underneath, pushing aside the camouflage. "How did this get here?" she cried out as she picked up the Cabbage Patch doll.

"I guess you just didn't see it," I replied, trying to look innocent.

She was so happy to get her doll that she didn't care how it arrived under our tree.

Making Happiness a Way of Life

Don't hang with people who tolerate you; instead, hang with people who celebrate you.

—Rev. Tadera L. White
New Hope Baptist Church
Birmingham, Alabama

Are you ready to make happiness a way of life? Do you want to look forward to each day with the confidence that you can achieve your goals? You may not be able to say yes to the second question just yet, but you must be able to say yes to the first one if you want to experience happiness.

Happiness is not an outfit you put on and take off. It's a way of being, thinking, and living day to day, every day. It may take small steps to achieve, but achieving happiness is worth the effort.

Many people just like you have created happy lives for themselves. Some of them were skeptical that they could ever be happy. If they overcame their fear and skepticism, so can you.

To attain happiness for yourself, consider adopting the habits shared by people for whom happiness is a way of life.

Treat your body like a temple, not a dumpster

Our bodies house all we need to function as human beings. We were designed to experience happiness. From our brain to every organ and system, we were created to be optimum living machines. We even have the drugs we need already inside of us, and our brain is the chemist ready to fill prescriptions as needed.

> *So many people spend their health gaining wealth, and then have to spend their wealth to regain their health.*
>
> —A. J. Reb Materi

Endorphins, which are three times more powerful at killing pain than morphine, are produced naturally by exercise, listening to soothing music, laughing, crying, and spending time in the sun.

Serotonin helps us have that happy feeling and controls our moods, aiding sleep and preventing depression. Bright light and exercise will increase our levels of serotonin.

Dopamine makes us energetic and alert and improves

our decision-making and socializing skills. Eating bananas, foods with antioxidants, almonds, and sunflower seeds are all believed to produce dopamine naturally.

Would you fuel your car with soft drinks and expect it to run? I don't think so. That's because you know your car was designed to run on gasoline (for now). Putting anything else in your car will not propel it forward and will likely ruin it.

Even though we have lots of information available about what is good for our bodies, many of us continue to shovel junk in there. Especially when we're young, we take our bodies for granted and tax them to their limits. Consuming unhealthy foods, neglecting exercise, shortchanging our sleep, and failing to drink enough water not only cause us to be overweight and lethargic, but also make us susceptible to illness, which in turn can diminish our happiness.

Because my sister Sonja died of multiple sclerosis in 2005, I always pause when I hear anything about this progressive and often fatal disease. One day I passed through the dining room as my youngest daughter was watching a video on her computer about multiple sclerosis. I stopped to listen to Dr. Wahls (2010) as she described how she had transformed her health and body after suffering for four years with secondary, progressive multiple sclerosis. When she was confined to a tilt-recline wheelchair, it became very hard for her to make her hospital rounds. Conventional medicine wasn't working. She was afraid she would be bedridden for the rest of her life. That's when Dr. Wahls began to study the research in auto-immune disease and brain biology. From what she learned, she decided to get her nutrients and vitamins from food rather than pills and supplements.

Using her Mitochondria Diet, Dr. Wahls recovered her ability to walk easily without a cane and ride her bicycle. Now she is devoting her life to lecturing and research. When she shared her story at a November 2011 TEDx talk, it went viral. Although she is careful to point out that her work has not been evaluated by the U.S. Food and Drug Administration and she does not promise to treat, prevent, or cure disease, she now uses these diets and protocols in her primary care and traumatic brain injury clinics.

You may not be ready to adopt Dr. Wahls' Mitochondria Diet, or any other organized eating plan, but your body will function better and help you maintain happiness when you do the following:

- *Cook and consume a diet of fresh fruits and vegetables.* Increasing concern for healthier eating and green living has resulted in better choices in major grocery stores and healthier choices in small and medium-sized stores.
- *Gain access to better-quality food.* At one time, it was difficult for low-income or more remote communities to have access to high-quality foods because of the absence or scarcity of grocery stores. But more and more communities of both high and low income levels are solving this problem

by setting up community gardens, engaging in community-supported agriculture, and attracting farmer's markets.

- *Make water your beverage of choice and consume at least eight glasses each day.* While there is disagreement over whether purified or filtered water is better than tap water, just choose your favorite and drink it regularly. It has become customary throughout the U.S.A. for commuters to carry a bottle of water with them.
- *Exercise at least three times a week.* Every day would be better. Walking is the easiest and least expensive exercise. Getting a walking buddy makes it more fun and more likely you'll be consistent..
- *Breathe deeply and consciously, sending oxygen throughout your body.* Deep breathing helps your body get rid of toxins and helps reduce stress.
- *Avoid sugar, caffeine, and alcohol.* Not only do these provide no nutrition, but all are addictive and can impair our motor and other skills. Because I've been a lifelong coffee drinker, I was surprised recently to discover that I'm not enjoying coffee as much as I once did. I think exercise and healthier eating are making coffee less welcome in my body and less satisfying to my taste buds.
- *Start your day with a healthy breakfast.* Not only is it the fuel that gets you going, but it also gives you energy, enables you to think better, and prevents you from binging, when you'll eat anything

to satisfy that late morning/early afternoon hunger.

- *Avoid eating after 7 p.m.* This one is a challenge for me because I admit I love to snack in the evening.

You certainly wouldn't trash a place you hold dear or for which you have reverence. You have been entrusted with the precious gift of a body. There is no one-size-fits-all when it comes to taking care of it. Invest time to research what combination of food, living habits, and exercise works best for you.

We spend a lot of time talking about attitudes, but without taking care of our bodies, we're missing a critical component. Take loving care of your body, and it will take care of you, resulting in the greatest benefit of all—happiness.

Ask for what you want

As a feng shui consultant finished a session with a client, she urged the client to write out what she wanted and post the list in her home. The client, who very much wanted to be married again, wrote *I want a husband* and posted it in every room of her house.

But when the consultant checked with her some time later, the client was very disappointed. She told the consultant that she kept getting asked out by married men. The consultant asked her what she had asked for. When she admitted that she'd asked for "a husband," the consultant pointed out to her that husbands were *exactly what she was getting.* The universe doesn't evaluate your wish and make suggestions. It just follows your directions.

Here's another story that illustrates the power of our words. A sixty-year-old couple went to a restaurant to celebrate their thirtieth wedding anniversary. A waitress with magical powers walked up to their table and said, "I will grant your wish. What do you want?"

The wife immediately said, "I'd like to go on a trip around the world with my husband." *Poof!* Two round-the-world tickets appeared in her hand.

The waitress with magical powers then turned to the husband and asked, "What do you want?"

He said, "I want a wife who is thirty years younger than I am." *Poof!* He was ninety years old.

Take small steps

Instead of frustrating yourself with the fact that some goals take time, think about what you can do today and what you can do tomorrow and what you can do the day after that to move an inch closer to that goal. I spent years longing to travel to Europe, for example. I browsed through travel magazines, read travel books, and watched travel shows. My friends patiently listened to my daydreams. Finally, one of them hit me with a key question: "Do you have a passport?"

All those years of longing to travel abroad, wishing I could save enough money for a trip, and I hadn't even taken the *very first step* to foreign travel: a passport.

Getting a passport was very much within my reach. Post offices and libraries make passports accessible. I didn't have to know where I was going to travel to apply. As a matter of fact, I discovered it's less stressful to obtain a passport before making any travel plans and while I was in no rush to receive it.

If I hadn't had the money to buy my passport immediately, I would have taken preliminary steps, like learning where to apply and picking up an application. Just learning what the passport fee is, is an important small step.

The Chinese proverb originated by Laozi is right: "A journey of a thousand miles begins with one step."

Widen your comfort zone

Many experts suggest that to achieve your goals, you may need to step outside your comfort zone. Instead of "stepping outside" your comfort zone, however, I prefer to think of it as "widening" my comfort zone. I feel as scared as the next person when I step outside my comfort zone. What could happen? I could fail. I could lose everything. I could get hurt.

True.

But I have a news flash for you. *Your comfort zone is not all that safe.* Horrors, failures, and disappointments can find you wherever you are, so why not have fun and enjoy your life along the way?

Something surprising happens when you step outside your comfort zone. Your old familiar zone widens, your world expands, your self-satisfaction increases, and your inner joy blooms.

But that's not all.

Stepping outside or widening your comfort zone is not only the path to growth and success, it also prevents stagnation and boredom. Perhaps you've always wanted to do something, but were afraid. We all are afraid when first facing a new or challenging experience.

Jeffers (1987) made it clear that we won't wake up one morning and suddenly find that we're fearless. That just isn't likely to happen. Your fear of the unknown never goes away, but you can't wait until you feel confident before you tackle the new challenge or risk. It's the other way around. People who achieve their goals work in spite of their fears. Then, as they discover that they can handle what comes up, their confidence grows.

You might be wondering why you should take *any* risks. Why not just stay where you are and play it safe? That may sound comforting at first, but the truth is that staying the same when something inside you wants to grow is painful. Some people wait until the pain of staying the same is greater than the pain of taking the risk before they change. Others wait until they are pushed out of their comfort zone by adversity or disaster.

Anna, for example, had created a life where her husband took care of all the business and she did the housekeeping, grocery shopping, and cooking. She had a job, but her husband either drove her to work or she caught the bus. She wanted to have more of a say in their affairs, but he was very demanding and she was very afraid. When her husband died of a heart attack, she found herself in charge of the gas station he owned. She had to manage the bills and decide what to do about his two trucks and their car. Since she had been content to let him chauffeur her around for so long, she didn't even know how to drive. She had never even written a check. Within a few days of his death, however, she was forced into change. She went from feeling helpless to learning how to be in charge of her life.

> *The first step toward success is taken when you refuse to be a captive of the environment in which you first find yourself.*
>
> —Mark Caine

Don't let bad news stunt your growth

Nonstop talk about the recession has a way of sucking us in. Even folks who are doing well financially, physically, and emotionally start to experience stress brought on by the fear of impending doom wrapped around the bad news. The greatest dangers of joining in the chorus of the downturn blues are that they distract us, blind us, and rob us. Here's how:

1. ***The news distracts us.*** It's a common human habit to focus on one thing at a time. Successful pickpockets count on it. Working in pairs, they may start a fight, causing you to look at them while one picks your pocket.

Or one bumps into you while the other deftly relieves you of your wallet.

Likewise, when you let the news of layoffs, store closures, and the national debt crisis dominate your attention; you are no longer focusing on your own success. Worst of all is when you choose to interpret the news as a scary reality that can only spell doom and gloom for you personally. When this happens, you can become mentally paralyzed by the *what-ifs*. If you're no longer taking action to reach your goals, your progress will indeed stall, and you'll soon be joining the legions who think the economy led to their personal downfall.

The ideal preparation would be to avoid being so vulnerable to these downturns by living simply and saving routinely. But many of us haven't taken these precautions, so what must we do now?

The most important thing to do is look at the positive side.

On Thanksgiving Day, one of my nephews announced that he had just been laid off. Instead of being morose, however, he was relieved. He had been working grueling hours—long days and weekends for months—in a stressful and negative environment. He was excited to finally have time off. Now he was going to turn his attention to seeking a way to get paid for his passion—creating beautiful art.

Sometimes the best positions to be in are the ones we've tried to escape. It's when your back is against the wall, your butt is against the cement, and you find yourself at the end of your rope that the most surprising feeling may be relief. When you're on the bottom there is only one way to go. Up.

This is not to say that there is joy in poverty. Absolutely not. But there is power in failure once we survive it. If in the aftermath we face what we really want to do with our lives, we can now invest all our energy and move successfully toward that deeply-held goal.

2. *The news blinds us.* When gas prices, taxes, or the cost of milk goes up, it's all over the news. But when prices go down, where's all the celebration on the news? When we focus on negatives, we miss seeing the good. And there's a lot of good in the world for us to see and be thankful for.

Every year, we seem to experience several devastating fires near where I live in Orange County, California. One fire came within only a few miles of my neighborhood. Every time there's a fire, we see people on TV news broadcasts whose homes were completely destroyed. They stand and stare at the ashes and sadly recount their failed efforts to save their homes. They mourn the loss of so many valuables. But there is usually one smiling couple hugging each other because they realize that they still have the most precious thing of all—each other.

Be grateful for the good in your life.

3. *The news robs us.* We choose how we view any event. What we focus on tends to multiply. When we choose to view the negative news about the economy as true and give it our attention, we are robbing ourselves of our energy. When our energy is diminished, we feel tired and listless. We lose time and finally we lose touch with our inner joy.

Don't let the downturn blues upend your life. Don't let the blues block your goals and activities and stunt your growth.

Stick to your goals. Revisit what works. Get back to the basics that make your life manageable.

When the economy appears to turn downward, it doesn't mean that people aren't spending. They're spending on different things, like information and training. If you create information products and services that can help people solve their problems, this is a time to promote what you offer.

If you lose your job, it may be time to try a new job or to return to school. Less disposable income causes us to trim away the fluff and focus on the absolute essentials. When home prices and interest rates drop, these can be viewed as opportunities for those who have wanted to buy, but couldn't afford to until now.

The one thing you must remember above all else is that the economy always turns, up or down. This period will pass, just as similar times in the past. When you refuse to allow the downturn blues to distract, blind, and rob you, and instead make positive moves toward your goal, you will later look back on this as a time when you experienced your greatest growth.

Practice positive thinking

Words have power. We all engage in self-talk, whether we want to admit it or not, using positive and negative words. According to research from the USC Laboratory of Neuro Imaging (http://www.loni.usc.edu/about_loni/education/brain_trivia.php), the average person has 70,000 thoughts per day.

The words we use in our thoughts are our interpretations of events and inner criticisms of our behavior. Some of these are conscious thoughts, the ones we are most aware of. Others are subconscious, below our level of awareness. They were programmed in us by our parents before the age of seven and are also based on our genetic makeup.

When we speak positive words at the conscious level, we create new ideas that work to change the subconscious programming. While Bruce Lipton (2007) was a professor of medicine at Stanford University, he discovered through stem cell research that when we change our perception, we make changes at the cellular level. Lipton echoes what spiritual leaders believe about the power of the mind over matter. Learn more about his work at http://www.brucelipton.com.

Our thoughts lead to our feelings, and our feelings determine how we behave. Since our thoughts are our way of interpreting the world, we are often guessing; yet we treat our thoughts as if they're true and accurate. If I notice a neighbor frowning as I pass by, for example, I may think that he or she disapproves of me. That could lead me to feel discouraged, which may lead me to feel uninspired and lacking in energy. That may cause me to neglect my writing and spend the day wallowing in self-pity.

But suppose my neighbor just had an argument with his spouse. Though he was looking in my direction, he was so distracted that he didn't even notice me. I have just allowed my misinterpretation of his behavior to negatively affect my whole day.

We're always interpreting what we see outside of us. We often harbor thoughts that are off base.

Since we're going to have thousands of thoughts in a day, and since these thoughts will lead to how we feel and behave, it's critical to work at keeping those thoughts positive. For all the talk about helping yourself with so-called positive thinking and repeating positive affirmations, some folks report that they've improved their lives without positive thinking and affirmations. The problem many of us have with positive thinking is we believe it means repeating affirmations to ourselves that we don't yet believe.

There are a few misconceptions about positive thinking: First, it isn't a quick-fix. No matter how many times you say, "I'm wealthy," you won't suddenly become wealthy without taking actions that lead to wealth. Second, it can blind us to reality. Newcomers to the concept of positive thinking believe it means to *ignore* the dark, dirty, and ugly parts of ourselves. If we do that, we'll find ourselves in a place called denial, and that leads to deeper problems. We must acknowledge our problems and dark thoughts, but at the same time we can't let them block us from taking positive action.

Positive thinking cannot prevent bad things from happening. You may think positive thoughts all day, but if you spill coffee on your computer keyboard, your computer may die—or your screen may turn a pukey pink. (Guess how I know that.)

Pavlina (2006) said, "Too much positive thinking can lead to self-delusion." He thinks that affirmations are worthless and that it's our intelligence that enables us to make progress in our lives. To be successful in our lives, we must learn to trust ourselves, face our fears, and heighten our awareness of the realities of our lives, such as our weaknesses.

While I agree with Pavlina that we must take responsibility for our lives, I believe that positive thinking followed by positive action aids us in taking responsibility and brings happiness into our lives.

Many folks report that positive affirmations don't work for them. To those folks, I must stress that affirmations don't replace action. They precede it. What you think about is what you bring about.

Whether you think you can or can't,
you're right.

—Henry Ford

Affirmations are self-talk. Regardless of your viewpoint on positive thinking, we all engage in self-talk. We all send many affirmations to our subconscious in a day, directing our behavior and results. If you practice saying positive affirmations, either silently or aloud, and you are experiencing difficulty in seeing what you're affirming manifested, perhaps you are making these four self-defeating mistakes:

1. *Stating what you don't want.* Your subconscious mind receives messages in about the same way children do. If you've ever told a child, "Don't eat this piece of cake," you know that they only hear the words that come after the "don't."

    The subconscious is completely neutral. It isn't capable of evaluating your affirmations to determine which are best. It just accepts what you say, whether it's positive or negative. Therefore, it's important that your affirmations state what you want, not what you don't want.

    Ineffective: I hope I don't have a car accident on my way to work.

    Effective: I am safe as I drive to work and arrive calmly.

2. *Stating in the future tense.* Setting your affirmation in the future makes it difficult to attain because the only time we can experience is the present. Create your affirmation using the first person with present-tense verbs.

Ineffective: I will become a good salsa dancer.

Effective: I am a smooth salsa dancer.

3. *Using vague words.* While becoming wealthy may be your goal, an affirmation like "I want more money" is not meaningful. A one-cent increase in your money is more, for example, but may not succeed in making you wealthy. Create straight, simple, specific affirmations.

   Ineffective: I want more money.

   Effective: I now have $10,000 in my bank account each month to pay my bills easily.

4. *Creating an affirmation you don't believe you can have.* One of the most powerful ways to manifest your goals through positive affirmations is to believe you deserve and can have whatever it is you want. You must be able to visualize what you want, see yourself having it, and experience the feeling of having it.

   Some people are able to achieve this through meditation; others, while dreaming or daydreaming. Others are helped by creating a "dream board" on which they post or glue clippings, drawings, or photos of what they want. Experiment with these techniques and find out what works for you.

   Ineffective: I now enjoy a monthly income of $100,000. (This affirmation, though well stated, won't work if you can't see yourself having this income.)

> Effective: I now enjoy a monthly income of $___________. (Be sure to specify an amount you believe you can have.)

Affirmations are not magic, although they may seem magical. They must be followed by action. Wherever you are in your life today is the result of countless affirmations you repeated to yourself in the past. Wherever you will be in the future will be based on the affirmations you repeat to yourself today. Avoid the four self-defeating mistakes to ensure that your affirmations manifest the positive life you desire.

One more thing about affirmations. When Noah St. John (2014), personal growth and professional development expert, was not seeing the results he wanted from his affirmations, he discovered that turning statements into questions led his subconscious to find the answers and change negative thought patterns into positive ones. He calls these *afformations*. To create an afformation, turn a statement like *I am rich* into a question, *Why am I so rich?* Learn more about this at http://noahstjohn.com/afformations/.

Park your mind in positive

Steve Simms (2011) contrasted our mind during sleep to a parked car. Unlike a parked car that stops running until we turn it on again, our mind keeps running in our sleep. To ensure that we wake up refreshed, in a good mood, and happy, he recommends "parking our minds in positive."

I don't think enough of us give credit to the value of sleep and the importance of what we plant in our minds before sleep. How do we "park our minds in positive" before we go to sleep? Steve suggests that consciously thinking positive and happy thoughts will enable you to wake up in a positive mood.

Here are some other tips to help you get the positive sleep you need.

1. *Get the right amount of sleep.* Experts say the average person needs between six and nine hours of sleep. To find out more about your own sleep needs, take one of the quizzes at the National Sleep Foundation's website, http://www.sleepfoundation.org.
2. *Make a sleep schedule and stick to it.* No matter what you may have heard, you can't catch up on lost sleep or save up for the future.
3. *Avoid caffeine and spicy foods before bedtime.* They interfere with sleep.
4. *Exercise in the afternoon to foster a good night's sleep. Taking a brisk walk, running, jogging, or engaging in other strenuous movement in the late afternoon contributes to a relaxing and restful sleep.*

Skip watching television as the last thing you do before sleep. In fact, remove the TV and other electronics from your bedroom. Create an atmosphere conducive to sleep so that when you go to bed, you signal your body that it's time for sleep. Instead, read a pleasant book, meditate, pray, or think of all the things you have to be grateful for as you ease into sleep.

Put your inner critic on time-out

I once asked my college students to raise their hands if they ever talk to themselves. Only a few tentative hands went up. Little did the students know, or want to admit, that *we all talk to ourselves*. All the time. This voice is called by many names. Most experts call it our inner critic.

I call mine Susie.

Susie likes to remind me of my failures and bring me down when I'm trying a new skill or meeting new people. Her goal is to dredge up sad, bad memories and deflate my self-worth. The first thing I do to disarm Susie is to acknowledge her presence. Then I insist that she sit down.

Susie is afraid of everything. Failure. Success. Riding. Driving. Flying. Speaking. Making mistakes. You name it, Susie's afraid of it.

Now you can understand that if I want to continue to achieve and enjoy, Susie must be acknowledged and silenced. But she can't be ignored. She can't be killed. Though our inner critic never goes away, we can, like cowboys taming a wild horse, bring this unruly voice under control. Horses are intelligent animals, and their behavior determines their survival in the wild. The cowboy (at least in the movies) succeeds in taming a horse not by yelling at the bucking horse from a safe place outside the corral, but by climbing on the struggling animal and staying aboard until the horse recognizes that all his kicking and bucking is counterproductive and becomes calm. (Relax, animal lovers. No animals were harmed during this metaphor.)

We can't ignore or wish away our own Susie. We must get the upper hand. As a matter of fact, getting our inner critic under control is the only way we can enjoy success and happiness. Left to her own devices, Susie would have me floundering in self-destructive behavior or cowering in a corner.

Some people think that positive affirmations can silence Susie, but we have to stop her in her tracks before the positive words can take hold. Sometimes I silence Susie gently; other times, I have to get firm and say, "Shut up!" She acts hurt and whines and slinks her way back to her corner, but I know it's an act. She'll be back to her old tricks the next time I step outside my comfort zone, try something new, or take a risk.

How are you handling your inner critic?

Listen to your intuition

Just as your inner critic has to be brought under control and silenced, so must your intuition be given more attention so it can guide you to your higher self, to the best life you were meant to live.

Intuition is knowing what is true and right without anyone telling you. When intuition puts you in touch with your higher self, you feel at peace and content, even in the midst of a difficult situation. Have you ever, even if for only a moment, felt more loving? Felt your own power and greatness? If so, you were in touch with your higher self.

Some people use other words for intuition. Hunches. The sixth sense. The still, small voice. Whatever you call it, we all have it, though it's better developed in some than in others thanks to practice.

Have you ever had a "hunch" to do something that worked out well for you? You probably couldn't explain the source of that thought, but you knew it was the right and good thing to do.

Perhaps you've heard of someone canceling a flight because he heard an inner voice that told him to do so.

Unfortunately, we've given our inner critic so much more attention that she drowns out our intuition. The best way to get in touch with your intuition is to shut off the inner chatter and the inner critic and get quiet. It's then that you can hear the still, small voice.

Sometimes this is tough to do without physically sitting still and shutting off all those thousands of thoughts that are racing through our heads every day. Some achieve quiet through meditation, others through self-hypnosis, and still others by listening to soothing music. Practicing getting to your higher self does not depend on your belief in any religion or deity; your intuition is without denomination. There are many meditation exercises that can guide you through the process of breathing properly to facilitate getting in touch with your intuition. The more you practice getting in touch with your intuition, the more you will be able to tackle the adversities that come your way, develop the relationships you desire, and create the inner joy and happiness you want.

Martha Beck (2001) recounted how, during her second pregnancy, she received precognitive flashes and intuitive experiences so vivid that she kept them secret from everyone. She came to realize that we all have intuitive knowledge in varying degrees. As we move closer to following our dream, she believes we awaken whatever "psychic" ability we have.

This was certainly true for me during several pivotal times in my life. One such time was when I had left my university position to start a tutoring business in my garage so I could be home with my fourth child. My business soon outgrew the garage and I began to fantasize about moving into a commercial building where I'd have a waiting room for parents, as well as separate classrooms where it would be comfortable for teachers to work with small groups of three students. The thought of finding the perfect place and being able to afford it seemed out of reach, but it occupied my mind night and day.

One day there was a detour on the route I usually drove to take my kids to their Montessori school. As soon as I was on the new street, I passed a brick building with a parking lot. (I have loved brick buildings since childhood.) From that day, I followed nudges inside me to approach the owners and negotiate for that building. Still I was nervous about making such a big financial move; my husband was petrified. One night while waiting for three students to complete a written assignment, the room got eerily quiet. Suddenly I heard a booming voice just like God spoke to Moses in the movie *The Ten Commandments*, except to me His voice said, "Go ahead and get your building." (No kidding!) Startled, I quickly looked around the room to see if the students had heard the voice too. Apparently they hadn't. With their heads still bent over their papers, they continued to finish their worksheets.

It was a long time before I shared this story with anyone, but I trusted this intuitive voice. Within months we had bought the building, which was more wonderful than I imagined. The previous owners even left the custom-designed waiting room furniture as part of the deal. My business thrived for two years in that building until my intuition propelled me to make another change.

To learn more about how your intuition works and complete some training exercises if you wish, I recommend you consult Beck (2001), Chapter 10.

SAY YES TO YOURSELF AND NO TO OTHER PEOPLE

Have you ever agreed to do something and two seconds later, knew you'd made a big mistake? Like the times you lend money to your cousin who never calls except to borrow money? Or the time your nomadic friend asked if he could spend the weekend with you just until he got his own place… and three days turned into three months? Or longer? Or the tenth time you went out of your way to take your child's forgotten lunch to school and now you're late to work again?

You can tell when you're about to be had. Or placed in a stressful situation. And yet you let it happen again. Or you do it to yourself.

Don't feel bad or blame yourself for falling victim to these situations or manipulative friends. I've been in these situations many times. That's what led me to my way of dealing with them.

If you want to be happy, you have to learn to say no to other people because then you're saying yes to yourself.

I've discovered that it feels so much better just to say no in the first place when you clearly don't want to do something. Saying no right away prevents later regrets. Here are some techniques that have worked for me.

- Keep it brief. The more you talk, the more it weakens your resolve. A firm no is enough.
- Don't apologize. You're not really sorry. Stick to the point.
- Don't engage in an explanation or excuse. It's nobody's business.
- Learn some pleasant, but true, alternate ways to say no if you're uncomfortable with the word "no." Smile while you say these other words.
    * Say, "I have other plans." (Maybe you have to paint your toenails.)
    * Say, "It's not a convenient time for me." (You planned to spend the evening enjoying quiet time.)
    * Say, "It's not a good time for me. Try back later." (When pigs fly.)

It's amazing how many of us feel compelled to answer the telephone, when it's completely our choice to do so. Here are some telephone tips:

- Look at Caller ID before picking up your phone. If it says Unknown Caller, let them remain unknown.
- If you recognize the name, but don't want to talk, don't pick up the phone. They'll leave a message. Or not. Or call back later. In this way, you respect your own time.
- When you pick up the phone, and it's a telemarketer, hang up—especially if he says, "May I speak to Mr. or Mrs. …" I know you were raised to be polite, but that doesn't apply to this situation.

I bet you already feel better just imagining yourself saying no in these situations. Now make it real. You'll be so glad you did.

> Color your life *calm* by choosing sky and ocean blue. Blue is the most popular color. That's probably because it's gender neutral and is believed to cause our bodies to produce chemicals that make us feel calm and sedate.

Summary

Making happiness a way of life begins with treating your body with reverence and respect. Invest time to research what combination of food, living habits, and exercise works best for you.

Happiness is not something you put on in the morning and remove at night. It is a way of living. It's the way you see the world and choose the experiences you want to have.

Four habits can help you create happiness in your life:

1. *Conceive and visualize what you want, but be careful what you ask for.* Remember, words have power.
2. *Set your goals without worrying about how you'll get there.* In other words, focus on what you want, not how and when it will appear.
3. *Chop your big goal into small manageable ones.* Think of small things you can do today or tomorrow that will begin to move you toward your goal.
4. *Instead of stepping out of your comfort zone, widen it to include new habits and experiences. One of the easiest ways to do this is to associate with others who are engaged in the activity that interests you.*

Don't let the news stunt your growth. Bad stuff is all around us, but it can be a dream killer if you dwell on it. Like all living things, the economy goes in cycles. It will be down, then go up, then go down again, and so on. Failure, though we try to avoid it, is also a natural part of life. Accept and learn from your mistakes and failures.

Though positive affirmations work for me, they don't always work for everyone. Thinking brings about results to fulfill it. What's important is to find a technique that brings about the results you desire.

While you may have trouble accepting the concept of positive thinking, consider other factors that researchers agree also lead to happiness: adequate sleep, a balanced diet, and exercise.

Finally, to make happiness a part of your daily life, bring your inner critic in line and enable your intuition to speak louder. Be good to yourself. Put your best interests first. Learn to say no to people and things that pull you away from your goals or deplete your positive energy.

HAPPINESS FLASHBACK

When Sonya, my second daughter, was a toddler, I asked her to hold onto a few pennies for a moment. When I looked at her again, she no longer had them in her hand.

"Where did you put those pennies?" I asked.

"In my pocket," she said in a matter-of-fact voice.

"What pocket?" I asked. Her shorts didn't have pockets.

"This pocket," she said, pulling out the waistband of her shorts and pointing to her panties. She had apparently decided that her panties made a handy pocket. I began to wonder how many things she had lost when they dropped out of her "pocket" without her even noticing.

Taking Responsibility for Your Happiness

Don't wait around for other people to be happy for you. Any happiness you get you've got to make yourself.

—Alice Walker

Waiting my turn in line at a popular coffee shop in San Diego, California, I listened to customers in front of me as they ordered breakfast:

"Breakfast quiche," said the first customer.

"I'll have the ham and cheese croissant," said the next customer.

"Do you want that for here or to go?" the server asked each time. Over and over, he asked the same question, "Do you want that for here or to go?"

That's when it hit me.

We answer that question every day when we make decisions about our lives.

Do you want happiness here or to go? Now or later?

We make daily choices about pursuing this or that goal or dream, or delaying our goal or dream for some future time. Unlike deciding to eat a croissant later, however, pushing our goals into the future may result in running out of time. We never get there. We never reach our goal. We never make our dream come true.

In a *Reader's Digest* article some years ago, a woman shared how she and her husband longed to take a trip around the world. Not wanting to go into debt to pay for the trip, they decided to save money for their trip so they could travel worry-free. Year after year, they socked away money in their dream vacation account. After ten years, they agreed that they had saved enough and eagerly made reservations to embark on their trip.

One week before they were to leave, the husband died of a massive heart attack.

As the wife grieved her loss, she also found herself deeply regretting that they had not made that trip earlier, even if it meant taking years to pay it off. She wrote the article to warn us not to delay our dreams.

We probably know people who feel unworthy of enjoying themselves during this lifetime, so they decide to delay their happiness for the afterlife. If you insist on believing that we are to suffer in this life, there may be nothing I can say to disrupt your belief. If you seek happiness in this life, however, continue reading.

How to get happiness here and now

Have you delayed a dream, a goal, or a desire until the time, circumstances, or money were right? There's nothing wrong with setting goals, making plans, and dreaming dreams. Unfortunately, there is seldom a right time other than now.

The problem is not acting immediately on our goals or dreams, even if the immediate action involves only small steps.

> *Many people think that if they were only in some other place, or had some other job, they would be happy. Well, that is doubtful. So get as much happiness out of what you are doing as you can and don't put off being happy until some future date.*
>
> —Dale Carnegie

If you are ready to get your happiness here and now, here are some ways to do it.

1. *Give yourself permission.* We are often our worst enemies as we wage wars with ourselves in our heads. If you find yourself hesitating to start toward a goal, that probably means you're afraid of success or failure. You are definitely concerned about whether you deserve the wonderful things you imagine.

   Maybe you're worried about what other

people think or are waiting for approval from others before you start. We all want the best for those we love. Learn to love yourself. Then give this amazing person called "you" permission to do and be and embrace whatever makes you happy.

2. *Find out what you really want.* This may sound simple on the surface, but discovering what we want requires research and exploration. We often judge what we want by the fun others seem to be having with it. You may think, for example, that you would enjoy living in a quaint cabin in the woods where you could spot a deer now and then, where you're off the main road and miles away from the nearest shopping center and the noise of the city.

   Is this really what you want? Explore this first by daydreaming the way you did as a child. Sit quietly and imagine yourself in the place, the situation, or the experience you think you want. Then check with your feelings. If you feel elated, energized, and excited, then you're on the right track.

   If, on the other hand, visualizing yourself having what you think you want makes you feel heavy, nervous, and uneasy, that means your feelings are warning you that pursuing this goal doesn't really hold the happiness you seek.

NOT SURE OF WHAT YOU WANT? SAMPLE FIRST.

When retailers offer free samples to consumers, it's a win-win strategy. For the retailer, he's making a very small investment in his business that may elicit a large return. For you? Without investing any money, you get to decide if you like the product. If you like the sample, you're more likely to buy it and recommend it to others. The store has landed a sale, created goodwill, and stimulated future sales. If you don't like the product, you haven't wasted any money and you're likely to still bear the store goodwill for this opportunity.

You can also engage in a sampling strategy before you make a major change by trying out a short or small example of what you want to do.

Before you pull up your city roots to relocate to operating a farm, for example, give this new lifestyle a test drive in the form of a vacation, a visit, or a short stay. While this living style may be very appealing from the comfort of a movie theater seat, it may not be what you really would enjoy in its entirety when you're there for an extended time.

Or perhaps you think you want to open a nonprofit organization. Volunteer to work in one first. You'll learn a lot about the inner workings, and you'll also see the operation in a different light. After getting a taste of it, you may discover that you don't like it after all. Or that it's a perfect fit.

Join an organization or trade association. If more than two people in the world are doing it, then there's probably an organization, a Facebook group, a convention, and a Tshirt. Check out groups in your interest and geographic area on http://www.meetup.com.

Before you make a big move or change, start reading about your interest. Learn all you can from books, articles, and the Internet. The benefits of this research are tremendous. You'll learn the vocabulary of the field, discover a wealth of sources to consult, and from the accounts of others learn what to expect. But be aware that travel brochures pale in comparison to the real-life experiences. Reading memoirs may also be helpful.

Sonia Marsh (2012) discovered a very different life from what she imagined when she, her husband, and their three sons relocated from a prosperous Southern California lifestyle to Belize in Central America. Hoping to bring her family closer in a slower-paced, tranquil paradise, she stepped out of the rat race… only to face creepy-crawly insects, storms, medical problems, and uneasy relationships with the locals. Worst of all, their employment plans began to slip away when they weren't able to get reliable Internet access. Fortunately, the family grew from their experiences, and even though they returned to Southern California after just one year, they are now clear that paradise is not a place, but a state of mind.

Gather the Resources You Need to Help You Reach Your Goals

Once you decide what you really want, it's time to line up the people, information, and tasks that will help you achieve your goal. When I decided to write this book, the following few steps helped me reach my goal:

- Read or heavily skimmed the major books, articles, and blogs in the happiness field.
- Bought a laptop.
- Attended a Positive Psychology conference to learn from researchers what findings they had discovered.
- Hired a life coach.
- Hired a publishing coach.
- Changed my main workspace to my living room picture window, where I could get more light.
- Visited the library and bookstores, sometimes to browse, sometimes to write in a different environment.
- Set up a writing schedule.
- Attended a publishing institute, where I met other authors actively involved in the writing process.
- Joined Toastmasters to work on my speaking skills.
- Joined an Internet marketing group to learn more about promoting my book.
- Kept notes on my experiences and observations on vacations and other trips away from home.

In addition to taking these (and many other) actions, I also had to accept my flaws and shortcomings. To help overcome these obstacles, I accessed inner resources such as prayer, meditation, and exercise to help me fight procrastination, bolster my confidence, and resist distractions.

Then, without condemning myself for not being perfect, I accepted my limitations and weaknesses and got help with making them work for me. Each one of these tasks played a part in moving from idea to successful completion.

LEARN FROM PEOPLE WHO HAVE ALREADY ACCOMPLISHED WHAT YOU WANT TO ACHIEVE

Decades ago, just one conversation with another mom who was working on her doctorate gave me the courage to begin my own doctoral studies. It's great to have a mentor or a supportive group with whom you can exchange ideas, but when you don't have one, seek out at least one person with whom to have conversations about your goal. Talk with someone who has achieved what you want to acheive.

Also hang out with people who do what you like to do or want to do. Before we plant new seeds, master gardeners advise us to prepare the environment by getting rid of any weeds, stones, and debris and preparing the soil. Likewise, when you decide to embrace happiness, you need to be in an environment that fosters happiness. To do that, you need to avoid people who will inhibit your growth and steal your joy. I know some of these folks may be your relatives, but my advice still stands. After all, your happiness is at stake.

> *If you want to fly like an eagle, then stop hanging out with turkeys.*
>
> —Richard Posner

Perhaps you want to do something but don't know anyone who enjoys doing that activity. Let's say you want to travel, but not by yourself. What can you do? Join a travel group or take a group tour. That's what I did.

In 2007, as soon as I retired from teaching, I signed up for a four-day workshop on going after your dreams. It was facilitated by Barbara Sher (2007). She called it a Scanner Retreat. Scanners are people like Leonardo da Vinci who have many talents and like to do lots of different things, some of which they never finish. The workshop was held in Ostuni, in the Puglia region of the southeast coast of Italy. When I thought about the fact that the retreat would be held in a remote location, I decided I also wanted to see the famous cities and locales of Italy while I was there. I decided to achieve two goals at once. I would go on a tour of the highlights of Italy the week before the workshop started, then enjoy the retreat.

The first thing I did was call my travel agent and tell her the dates I had in mind. She booked me on an eight-day tour. There were about forty people on the tour, mostly couples and about five singles. At the start of the tour, I didn't know any of the other vacationers, but we had a common interest in enjoying Italy. We traveled from Rome to Florence, Tuscany, Pisa, and Venice, soaking up the culture, food, music, history, and the captivating atmosphere unique to Italy.

Once my eight-day tour ended, I had a six-day gap before the Scanner Retreat was to begin. How was I going to fill that time?

In talking to one of my friends months before the trip, we discovered that we would both be in Rome during those six days. She would just be starting her tour of Rome and I would be finished with mine. We decided to stay in the same hotel and rendezvous for dinner every evening when she returned from her tours. During the day, I explored the neighborhood and surroundings on my own and stayed away from the typical tourist spots.

At the end of the six-day gap, I flew from Rome to Ostuni to begin the Scanner Retreat, the original event that had lured me to Italy. Barbara Sher could have set her seminar anywhere in the world, but presenting the activities in the courtyard of a centuries-old *masseria* (a wine-producing estate that formerly had animals, olive groves, and many buildings) elevated the experience. A few of the attendees were from Europe, but most of us were from the U.S., mostly Californians. During that trip, I gained a new batch of friends, all of us on the same path to leading fulfilling lives. A year later, a number of us enjoyed a reunion in Los Angeles.

SET THE GOAL FOR WHAT YOU WANT WITHOUT WORRYING ABOUT HOW YOU'LL GET THERE

You must have a vision of where you want to be when you succeed. The details of how to get there will unfold as you go. Here's an example of how this worked for me.

For years, I'd wanted to remodel my kitchen and family room to make them more user-friendly. I visualized what life would be like in my new space. But since I was just coming out of a period of financial setback, I wasn't even sure if I could land the refinancing loan I needed. Nevertheless, with my vision clearly in mind, I boldly applied for the loan. And I got it! The contractors and my project all fell into place, and in record time, too.

Along the way, I heard nothing but horror stories from friends and coworkers who had undergone remodeling projects. But I refused to allow their experiences to determine mine. When my remodeling was finished, many of those people of course asked me how it went. When I said it was a wonderful experience, every single person asked me how I did it. How did I do it? I decided in advance that I was going to have *an easy and positive experience*. The remodeling was finished on time, and I had money left over.

More than once in the past, I used the *law of attraction* without realizing it. That is, I always believed that positive thoughts helped bring positive results. When the movie based on *The Secret* by Rhonda Byrne was released in 2006, it swept across the world, inspiring many, but upsetting others, who saw it as bogus, drivel, and downright useless. The movie consisted of a series of interviews of individuals from fields such as quantum physics, psychology, metaphysics, and theology. The various speakers set forth the idea that you can attract what you want by believing in and holding positive thoughts about it. Although the movie never explicitly promoted the law of attraction, viewers gave it credit for doing so. Skeptics dismiss the law of attraction as being modern pseudo-religion with no scientific foundation and like to point to what they believe follows from the premise: any illness or catastrophe we experience is our fault. Those who embrace the law of attraction don't see it as new at all. They find the same belief in the Buddha's teaching that "the mind is everything. What you think you become." And in Christian tradition, "if you can believe, all things are possible to him who believes" (World English Bible).

Going beyond the focus on material gain that some believe is stressed too much in the law of attraction, Wayne Dyer (http://www.drwaynedyer.com/), author of more than thirty books on mind/body/spirit, has been frequently quoted as saying that we attract not what we want, but what we are. I agree with him; when we live in a place of God-consciousness, the universe will give us more of that. But when we live in a place of ego-consciousness, we get more of that instead and thus are never fulfilled. There's nothing wrong with having desires and goals, as long as we are not tied to the outcome.

CHOP YOUR BIG GOAL INTO SMALLER, MANAGEABLE ONES

If you're like many people, you may have trouble visualizing a big dream. Even if you aspire to becoming a millionaire, owning a beachfront villa, running a successful business, or traveling the world, you may not be able to see it just yet.

No amount of mental calisthenics can help you reach goals if you can't visualize or believe you can achieve them. So why not set a series of small, reachable goals that move you toward your big goals?

Approach it the same way you eat a steak (sorry, vegetarians, but work with me here). There's no doubt you can finish that sizzling steak on your plate, but you wouldn't try to get the whole thing down in one big bite. You have to cut it into pieces and eat them one at a time.

BE WILLING TO DO WHAT IT TAKES TO REACH YOUR GOAL

Now this may sound too obvious even to mention, but it's true. Many years ago, when my kids watched *Mister Rogers' Neighborhood*, an American children's TV series that began in the 1960s, one of his popular songs was "You've Got to Do It." The gist of this seemingly simple song was that you can make believe, wish, or daydream about what you want, but for something to happen you've got to take action. In other words, after planning, visualizing, and setting goals, you still have to *take action*.

Do you want to reach goals or make changes in your life? Are you willing to do what it takes?

—John Addison

It's often fun to find friends to join you in activities. There will be times, however, when no one is available to join you on your journey to your goal. It's at those times when what it takes to reach your goal is to be willing to go it alone.

Here's an experience that demonstrates what happens when you are willing to do what it takes. One weekend a few years ago, I went to see the musical *The Color Purple* at a theater in downtown Los Angeles with a group of theater-goers from Santa Ana College in Orange County. We parked our cars at the college and went by charter bus into L.A. I chose to go with this group so I wouldn't have to drive.

As we made our way to our seats, I was disappointed to see that we were in the highest balcony. You know—up in the "nosebleed" section. Whoever designed that steep slope of a balcony must never have had to sit up there. I'm not squeamish, but I was beginning to realize that I was not going to enjoy this musical so many miles from the stage. The actors would probably look about three inches tall. It was twenty minutes before the curtain went up, and I was so discontented that a feeling of not settling for less than I deserved welled up inside me. Different scenarios and dialogues started shouting in my head. This was the internal argument between the two inner me's:

> *I refuse to sit in these inadequate seats.*
>
> *Who do you think you are? Everyone else seems to be okay, even though they're complaining about how high up these seats are.*
>
> *That's them. I'm not happy.*
>
> *What are you going to do about it? The show's about to start.*
>
> *I don't know. But there's no way I'm going to enjoy the show in this seat! I wonder whether they have any available seats left in the lower levels.*
>
> *Go and see. Are you willing to spend more money on another seat?*
>
> *Yes, I'm willing to buy another seat. I'm going to the box office and buying a seat in the orchestra. Or at least the mezzanine.*
>
> *What if they don't have any seats left?*
>
> *If they don't have any available seats, I'll just call a friend to come and pick me up. I'd rather hang out in the lobby than sit in this seat!*
>
> *You mean you're willing to make all those folks between you and the aisle get up to let you out?*
>
> *Yep. I'm outta here!*

I rose from my seat and slid my way to the aisle, murmuring, "Excuse me, excuse me, excuse me." As I approached the ticket booth outside the theater, a lady walked up to me.

"Do you need a ticket for this performance?" she inquired.

"Where's the seat?" I asked, looking at the ticket in her hand to verify that it was a better section than I'd been in.

"The mezzanine," she replied.

"Great! Are you trying to sell it or give it away?" I had to check.

"You may have it for free because my friend couldn't come," she said.

"Thank you."

She placed the ticket in my outstretched hand. I felt very satisfied, but now I wanted to try to give away my top balcony seat if I could. I began scanning the approaching crowd, trying to spot anyone headed to the ticket booth. Just then, a gentleman approached me and extended a ticket toward me. "Would you like a free ticket to today's performance?" he asked. "My wife couldn't attend."

"Where's the seat?" I inquired a second time. By this time, I definitely wasn't going to settle for a bad seat.

"Oh, it's a great seat," he insisted, practically begging me to accept his free ticket. "It's in the orchestra."

"Thanks!" I scooped the ticket out of his hand.

Now I had three tickets to this performance.

Although I tried to give away my two extra tickets, I found no takers. And by now, security had their eyes on me, trying to decide if I was a scalper. It was now less than ten minutes before curtain, so I gave up trying to give away my extra tickets and dashed to my wonderful new orchestra seat.

I enjoyed the performance immensely in my wonderful seat, only eleven rows from the stage. I saw every nuance of the casts' telling facial gestures and the lively conducting of the orchestra leader. The stirring vocal and dance performances and heartwarming story were made even better by my proximity to all the action.

I am positive that I would not have attracted this great seat into my life if I had not first been willing to do whatever it took.

Please note that I didn't have to take any of the drastic actions that played out in my head. I just had to be willing to do them.

When you refuse to accept what you *don't want*, declare with passion what you *do want* and are willing to do whatever it takes to get it, the universe conspires to bring what you want and place it in your hands.

Do more of what you enjoy

It's inevitable that as we get older, we will attend more funerals. There's nothing that reminds us of our own mortality like watching our friends and contemporaries succumb to illnesses or die of natural causes. One of my friends uses funerals to remind herself to keep busy enjoying her life. "Every time I return from a funeral," she says, "I book another cruise."

You may not long for cruises, but surely there's something you've always wanted to do. If you don't do it now, when are you going to do it?

Maybe you've always wanted to pursue a certain hobby, write your life story, climb a mountain, travel by rail across the United States, or learn another language. The possibilities are endless.

But I can already hear your objections:

- I don't have the money.
- I don't like traveling alone.
- I don't know anyone to go with me to [fill in the blank].
- I'm too old to [fill in the blank].
- I'm afraid to fly.
- I'm afraid to drive.
- I don't like public transportation.

For just a moment, pretend that none of your objections exist. What would you love to do? Make a list. Since this is all imaginary, feel free to make your list as long as you want and make your wishes as elaborate as you can imagine!

Now look at your list and pick one wish and write all the things you would have to do to have that wish come true for you.

I'll give you a personal example. I mentioned that

one of my goals was to travel to Europe. What did I need to do?

- Get a passport.
- Choose a country.
- Look up airfares.
- Look up organized tours going to that country.
- Check out prices of tours.
- Select a tour.
- Investigate and rearrange my finances to see how I could comfortably afford the trip.
- Talk to people who have been where I want to go to get tips and advice.

Your next step is to make a list of each of the items on your list, and for each item identify what you need to do to accomplish your goal. For example, to get a passport I needed to find out:

- Where to get a passport
- The price of a passport
- The application process
- What else is involved

By the time you get to this third tier of your list, you will see that there are things you can do today or tomorrow. For example, it takes only a few minutes to find out where to get a passport. If you have access to the Internet, you can find out all you need to know about passports (or anything else) very quickly. If you don't have access to the Internet, your local library does. The librarian will be happy to help you find the information you need.

This is just the start, of course. But keep it up and your objections will begin to evaporate. Get busy, and start on your first list now!

Be willing to fail or quit

Our unwillingness to fail or be rejected is what causes us to procrastinate or stick with things longer than we should. We keep holding back, waiting for things to be perfect. We cling to a failing project long after it's dead. It's wiser to research and think things through, but you must also let these ideas, projects, or activities be born, no matter what the outcome.

I decided long ago that when I'm sitting in my rocking chair, sporting my chic gray hairstyle and recounting my life story, I'd much rather talk about the many things I tried that didn't work out than about the many things I wanted to do but never had the courage to try.

Seth Godin (2007) pointed out that successful people quit many times. The key is knowing when to quit before you spend a disproportionate amount of time and energy on a goal or task that's not going anywhere.

Don't let fear of failure make you hesitate to start a project. Don't think of quitting as failure; think of it as the cost of succeeding. Set your vision and be willing to do whatever it takes to get there. The "how" will unfold in wonderful and amazing ways.

> *Do not dwell in the past, do not dream of the future, concentrate the mind on the present moment.*
>
> —The Buddha

GET IN THE FLOW

Have you ever concentrated so hard on what you're doing that time seems to stand still? Csikszentmihalyi (1990) noted that being so much in the flow of a project is a time of optimal experience. When you are in the flow, you get so fully absorbed in what you're doing that you forget about time and your surroundings. Best of all, you become most creative and productive during these times. You feel serene, completely unaware of others around you, and so unaware of physical needs that you may even forget to eat.

When I'm engaged in writing an article or a blog (or this book), I sometimes get so caught up in what I'm thinking that my fingers seem to fly across my keyboard as I try to capture the thoughts rushing out of my head. At these times, I reach such a peak of exhilaration and joy that I forget to eat (or do anything else). When this peak period subsides, however, my stomach growls to remind me of my neglect.

Although flow doesn't usually occur when you're just beginning to learn a new task, you'll know right away if you like the activity. You're naturally drawn to activities where you can use your strengths and that appeal to your tastes. It's after you've practiced this activity and gained a level of mastery that you begin to experience the exhilaration, satisfaction, and timelessness that we call flow.

When you're in the flow, you're single-tasking, not multi-tasking, where you're paying half-attention to menial tasks. Flow is concentration at its best. To get into the flow and be able to enjoy its by-product, happiness, you will need to

- Pick a task you enjoy for the sheer pleasure, not its income potential, even though it may result in increased income.
- Remove outer and inner distractions, giving yourself a conducive workspace and a clear mind.
- Choose to do this task during your peak time of day.
- Choose a task that's challenging, but not too difficult.
- Practice, practice, practice.

Summary

You are responsible for your own happiness. Regardless of your circumstances, you are faced with daily choices that either propel you toward your goals, discourage you, or delay your progress.

It all begins with giving yourself permission to move toward a happier life. Once you've done this, you must find out *what you really want*. If you're not sure what you want, or you have difficulty visualizing it, experiment with the life you imagine by, for example, planning an extended stay or taking a volunteer position before committing to a long-term arrangement.

Once you've decided what you want, set goals and gather as many resources as possible to help you make the change. This includes finding supportive people who can help you. Some of these will be people who have already achieved what you want to achieve. Others will be people who believe in your dream and are eager to help you attain it.

When setting your goal, focus on the *what* but not the *how*. Once you're clear and enthusiastic about your goal, expect people to show up and opportunities to open up to help you.

Chop your goals into small manageable pieces and be willing to do what it takes to reach your goals.

Once you've discovered the activities and experiences you enjoy, plan more of them.

As you go after your goals, it's inevitable that you'll encounter setbacks, delays, and failures. These are educational experiences. Take the risks to pursue your goals, even if you decide later to abandon them to pursue new ones.

Finally, make it a goal to find activities that are so enjoyable that you forget the passage of time, and enjoy increased creativity and productivity.

My mother saw this 1910 poem by Rudyard Kipling as a call to responsibility, resilience, and positive mental attitude. It became one of my favorites, too.

If

Rudyard Kipling

If you can keep your head when all about you
Are losing theirs and blaming it on you;
If you can trust yourself when all men doubt you,
But make allowance for their doubting too;
If you can wait and not be tired by waiting,
Or being lied about, don't deal in lies,
Or being hated, don't give way to hating,
And yet don't look too good, nor talk too wise:

If you can dream, and not make dreams your master;
If you can think, and not make thoughts your aim;
If you can meet with Triumph and Disaster
And treat those two imposters just the same;
If you can bear to hear the truth you've spoken
Twisted by knaves to make a trap for fools,
Or watch the things you gave your life to, broken,
And stoop and build 'em up with worn-out tools;

If you can make one heap of all your winnings
And risk it on one turn of pitch-and-toss,
And lose, and start again at your beginnings
And never breathe a word about your loss;
If you can force your heart and nerve and sinew
To serve your turn long after they are gone,
And so hold on when there is nothing in you
Except the Will which says to them: "Hold on!"

If you can talk with crowds and keep your virtue,
Or walk with kings, nor lose the common touch,
If neither foes nor loving friends can hurt you,
If all men count with you, but none too much;
If you can fill the unforgiving minute
With sixty seconds' worth of distance run,
Yours is the Earth and everything that's in it,
And, which is more, you'll be a Man, my son!

HAPPINESS FLASHBACK

My husband was usually easy-going and soft-spoken, in sharp contrast to my occasional histrionics. But one time when the kids were engaged in a high-pitched argument, my husband lost his composure. "CONTROL YOUR TEMPER!" he shouted. We all turned to him and burst into laughter. We still get a kick out of the irony of it.

Simplifying Your Life for Happiness

Most of the luxuries and many of the so-called comforts of life are not only not indispensable, but positive hindrances to the elevation of mankind.

—Henry David Thoreau

In the movies of my childhood about the westward migration of Americans in the 1800s, there was always a string of rickety wagons loaded with families' worldly possessions slowly crossing the prairies. Bed frames and rocking chairs were tied on top with pots and pans clanging against the sides. Drawn to what they hoped would be a more prosperous life on cheap land they'd heard about in letters from relatives and friends who had gone before, the pioneer families pushed on in spite of dwindling supplies, wagon breakdowns, and occasional fights with frustrated and cantankerous fellow pioneers along the way.

As the movie family grew weary of fighting off disease, battling with Native Americans who were desperately trying to protect their land and families, stopping only to bury those on whom the trip had taken its toll, plus trying to keep up their spirits, they eventually realized they could travel faster if they lightened their load. The western migratory trails became lined with discarded household furniture and other possessions.

> *You have succeeded in life when all you really want is only what you need.*
>
> —Vernon Howard

While the pioneers shed their possessions to expedite their westward journey, throughout history, people have chosen simple living for spiritual, secular, health, anti-consumerism, and other reasons.

> *He has the most who is most content with the least.*
>
> —Diogenes

Simple living has deep historical roots. Diogenes of Sinope (fourth century BCE), believed that happiness comes from meeting our basic needs. He is credited with many witticisms regarding simple living. Thoreau (2013), American author, poet, abolitionist, and naturalist (born in

1817 in Concord, Massachusetts), conducted a two-year experiment with simple living in a cabin he built beside Walden Pond and wrote about the experience in *Walden* in 1854. Mohandas K. Gandhi, born in India in 1869, is best known for non-violent civil disobedience and living a simple life of self-sufficiency.

Many ordinary people today are throwing up their hands in defeat, trying to keep up with the Joneses at the cost of amassing huge debts. They have engaged in a "simplicity movement" to reduce stress and become participants rather than bystanders in their lives. The possessions we craved in the past, such as luxury cars, expensive wardrobes and accessories, and a big house with a big backyard, have betrayed us. The satisfaction we expected from our expensive possessions is short-lived. Our sense of well-being also declines as we see the cost of keeping up our possession-rich lifestyle becoming too high.(Stutzer & Frey, 2004)

Putnam (2000) found these efforts to keep up with the Joneses by commuting to higher paying jobs disturbing, not just for what it does to our personal lives, but for what it means to our community. Those of us who have been freeway fliers making long commutes to work didn't need Putnam to tell us those commutes are killers.

Dirksen (2011) found that every ten minutes of commuting results in 10 percent fewer social connections. Commuting adds to social isolation and is destined to contribute to unhappiness.

I'm a former road warrior. Trust me—you do not ever

get used to the commute. It's not the miles that get you down. In my case, it was the uncertainty brought on by changing weather, the rising cost of gas, and accidents and detours that persuaded me to move closer to my job. After driving thirty-five miles one way to work the first year of my last full-time job, it wasn't long before I vowed to move closer. Yes, it meant selling my house and uprooting my kids, and getting settled into a new lifestyle. But my peace of mind depended on it. When I found a house eight and a half miles from my job, I was elated. For the first time in my married life, I could be home in minutes, easily attend my kids' school events, and even walk to the store, the post office, and other places if I chose to do so.

Americans' fascination with cars has diminished so much in our nation. In fact, the less time we have to spend in them, the happier we are. A major consideration for families considering a move is the "walk score" of the location, which you can find for your home and workplace at http://www.walkscore.com/. The more errands, socializing, and civic engagement that can be accomplished on foot, the higher the walk score.

More than just a reaction to economic conditions, simpler living is enabling families to spend more time together. Parents can read to their kids at night. We worry less about bills and upkeep. On a practical level, moving to a smaller dwelling also means less to store and clean. People who can downsize without feeling deprived can better enjoy the possessions that have high value for them.

Many of us find we are happier when we simplify our

lives. But many of us are also like the American tourist in the following story, which is similar in spirit to the thinking of the Chinese philosopher, Chuang Tzu.

> An American tourist stood at the pier of a small coastal Mexican village and watched as a small boat with just one fisherman docked. Inside the small boat were several large yellowfin tuna. The tourist complimented the Mexican fisherman on the quality of his catch and asked how long it had taken to catch them.
>
> "Only a little while."
>
> "Then why didn't you stay out longer and catch more fish?" the tourist asked.
>
> "With this," the fisherman said, "I have more than enough to support my family's needs."
>
> "But what do you do with the rest of your time?"
>
> The fisherman said, "I sleep late, fish a little, play with my children, take a *siesta* with my wife, Maria, and stroll into the village each evening. I sip wine and play guitar with my *amigos*. I have a full and busy life."
>
> The tourist scoffed. "I can help you. You should spend more time fishing and use the proceeds to buy a bigger boat. With the proceeds from the bigger boat, you could buy several boats. Eventually, you would have a fleet of fishing boats. Instead of selling your catch

to a middleman, you could sell directly to the processor and open your own cannery. Then you would control product, processing, and distribution. You could leave this small village and move to Mexico City, then to Los Angeles, and eventually to New York, where you could run your ever-expanding enterprise."

"But, how long will this take?" the fisherman asked.

"Fifteen to twenty years."

"But what then?" asked the fisherman.

The tourist laughed. "That's the best part. When the time is right, you would sell your company stock to the public and become very rich. You would make millions!"

"Millions? Then what?"

"Then you would retire," the American said. "Move to a small, coastal fishing village, where you would sleep late, fish a little, play with your kids, take a *siesta* with your wife, and stroll to the village in the evenings, where you could sip wine and play your guitar with your *amigos*."

Do you, like the American tourist in the story, long for a simpler life, but believe you can only have it in some distant future? The truth is, of course, that you can have it now. You can use one or more of the following ideas to simplify your life and enjoy it more every day.

SLOW DOWN

Since the beginning of the Industrial Era in our country, we seem to have become obsessed with doing things faster and faster. Have you almost been sideswiped by a grocery shopper rushing to beat you to the checkout line? Or was that you who whizzed by me?

Our lives are so rushed, it's a wonder we even see the scenery as we go through life. Oh, that's right—we don't.

Penelope Green (2008), shared Honoré thoughts on slow as a state of mind.

> Fast isn't turning us into Masters of the Universe. It's turning us into Cheech and Chong.... Slow is just a new word to understand old problems.... It's a refreshening of ideas that have been there since time immemorial. But there's a new appeal about the word slow. It's pithy, it's countercultural.

The slow movement began in Italy in the 1980s as the Slow Food Movement. Now "slow" is a term used to encourage us to do everything at the right speed, whether it's education, exercise, sex, or work. The slow movement isn't "anti-speed." It favors connectedness. Rushing through everything prevents us from savoring food, enjoying life experiences, and associating with people. Honoré doesn't suggest that we slow our lives to a snail's pace. But he finds it troubling that we have one-minute children's stories, speed dating, and the need to amass thousands of so-called friends on Facebook, each of which diminishes the opportunity for a meaningful encounter.

If you always feel tired and rushed and can barely remember what you did, ate, or saw in a day, then you know you need to slow down. It's no surprise that the Slow Food Movement began in Italy, the home of fabulous food. When Carlo Petrini learned that McDonald's planned to build a franchise near the Piazza di Spagna in Rome, he organized a demonstration. As weapons of protest, he and his followers threw—what else?—penne pasta. Soon after, Petrini founded the International Slow Food Movement, which encourages us to take care with what and how we eat. The Slow Food Movement's advocates want to save endangered foods such as the red abalone, Northern California heirloom turkeys, and Vella Cheese Company's dry, aged Monterey Jack cheese, promote responsible agricultural systems, and help us return to the joy of food preparation and consumption.

If you're ready to slow down, here are some ideas to get you started:

- Avoid cookie-cutter homes by visiting http://slowhomestudio.com.
- Enjoy your travel. Wrap yourself in sustainable clothes, jewelry and furniture at http://alabamachanin.com.
- Disenchanted with instant messaging? Try the slow electronic mail movement at http://www.slowlab.net/.

- Read Honore (2005) *In Praise of Slowness: Challenging the Cult of Speed*
- Learn more about the Slow Movement at http://www.carlhonore.com/.

Investigate these ideas on slowness. The slow life may be just your speed.

Instead of Texting, Send Letters or Cards

Have you noticed that even people who don't like to send letters admit that they love to receive them? Handwritten personal letters build relationships in a way no other communication can.

When my children were young, they grumbled when I insisted that they send handwritten thank-you notes for every Christmas and birthday gift they received. From the way they moaned and whined, you'd think they'd grow up hating to send thank-you notes. On the contrary, now they even send a written thank-you to each member of the interview committee following job interviews.

In addition to handwritten letters, I also like to send "real" greeting cards for holidays when people least expect them. Until she received one from me, one friend said she didn't even know they made Thanksgiving greeting cards. You can buy a set of six or eight of these cards for almost every holiday for under $5. It only takes a few minutes to address them, and mail carriers will even pick up your outgoing mail when they deliver your incoming mail.

Every Christmas, I share highlights of my family's

year in poetic form, print it on holiday paper, and include it with a picture of the family in my Christmas cards. Not only does this delight my friends and family, but it has given me quite a collection of memories of things I would have forgotten over the years.

I also enjoy sending postcards when I travel. To make this task easier, I print address labels before I leave home. On the first day of my trip, I look for affordable postcards, and then, when I have a long ride or some downtime, I jot a brief greeting on each card. If I don't find a post office handy, I ask hotel guest services to get the stamps and mail them for me.

The greatest thing about letters, especially personal, handwritten ones, is that they create double happiness, touching the sender and the receiver. We can get encouragement and guidance from these two heartwarming letter-writing projects.

Heartfelt letters create enduring bonds of appreciation

Lynette M. Smith, copyeditor and owner of All My Best (http://goodwaystowrite.com), is on a mission to restore the art of showing our feelings of appreciation through letter writing. She believes that even simple expressions of appreciation can return our world to joy and hope, one relationship at a time.

Smith (2012) told her personal story to illustrate how her book came about.

> On November 21, 2008, my husband and I attended the wedding rehearsal dinner of our son, Byron, and his fiancée, Rachael. That evening, they surprised us when the two of them each made a special presentation to their respective parents–a beautifully framed, one-page heartfelt letter. Their best man and maid of honor read the letters aloud as Byron and Rachael each stood beside their own parents. Each letter described what they had treasured about growing up in their family, what they had especially appreciated about each parent, and what values they had learned and planned to bring to their marriage.
>
> We were deeply moved—all of us: four parents, bride and groom, and the rest of the guests. And I can tell you, those framed letters will always hold a place of honor in our homes. To this day, whenever I tell someone about that night and our treasured letters, my hand automatically moves to my heart. That's where I still feel the experience. And my love and appreciation for our son who expressed his love and appreciation for my husband and me so beautifully has truly strengthened the bonds we already felt.

Smith's three-part reference book addresses milestone birthdays; special occasions for school, military, romance, family, rites of passage and career; and professional and personal relationships, including aging, eulogies, and mending relationships. A special bonus is her selections of positive words, inspirational quotes, and sentence jumpstarts.

Handwritten love letters to strangers can bring you and them back from despair

Hannah Brencher, a copywriter and creative consultant, was fortunate to have a mother who communicated via handwritten letters rather than the more efficient, but less touching, email and text messaging. Hannah shares at http://hannahbrencher.com/about/ the story of how she got into the business of broken hearts. And be sure to watch the video at http://on.ted.com/Brencher to hear Hannah's story in her own voice. If you feel inclined to join her global letter writing campaign, you can do so at http://www.moreloveletters.com/.

Showing gratitude by writing and mailing thank-you notes is a habit that happy people practice. The best thing about sending personal handwritten letters is not only do you make someone's day—but you make your own day, too.

Repeat a favorite scripture, affirmation, or saying

I mentioned earlier that one of my favorite scriptures, which I recite daily upon rising, is "This is the day which the Lord hath made: let us rejoice and be glad in it" (Psalm 118:24 NASB).

For year-round encouragement, consider a book by Breathnach (2009) which offers 366 essays, one for every day of the year, and encourages taking mental and spiritual inventories of your life. Though directed at women, the wisdom, tips, and ideas in the book can be used by women and men alike who want to live authentic daily lives. Each essay begins with a relevant quote, and the essays are woven with six threads of abundant living: gratitude, harmony, order, beauty, joy, and simplicity. Many of the ideas proposed in the book are simple. "Clean out your closet." "Be grateful for what you have." They're so simple and obvious, in fact, that you may be tempted to discount them. But these are some of the very simple habits identified by happy people in research studies and surveys.

Here's your chance to be part of happiness research.

We've been sharing findings of happiness research throughout the book. If you'd like to be part of the research, grab the iPhone app Mappiness, created by the London School of Economics. It will contact you a few times a day to ask you to rate your mood. It will enter your response with data about your location and environment. The information is collected to see how our happiness is affected by our local environment. Researchers at the London School of Economics will be publishing the results. In the meantime, you can consult the app to see how you are ranking on happiness over time. Get the app at http://www.mappiness.org.uk/. Since this is a UK project, George MacKerron, the project leader, indicates he may not use results from outside the UK, but you can still participate to gauge your own happiness levels.

Laugh!

We 21st-century Americans spend an enormous amount of money on doctors, medicine, and medical treatments. It's too bad many of us haven't grasped a truth set forth throughout the ages: *Laughter is the best medicine.* If you don't believe this, treat yourself to a deep, robust, belly laugh and notice how much better you feel.

Laughter is more than a mood enhancer. It actually has health benefits. It can reduce stress, strengthen your immune system, improve your memory, and increase your intellectual performance. Bernie Siegel (1998), a retired pediatric surgeon and author, went as far as to say that happy people generally don't get sick.

Dr. Madan Kataria believed so much in the benefits of laughing that he started Laughter Yoga and Laughter Clubs. Kataria says that laughter is nature's stress-buster. There are more than six-thousand Laughter Clubs in sixty countries. To learn about his clubs and conferences, visit his website at http://laughteryoga.org/english.

Need more reasons to laugh? Goodheart (1994) shared how to use laughter for healing and making connections. Researchers have studied what happens in the body when we laugh. Learn more at http://holisticonline.com/.

Time spent laughing is time spent with the gods.

—Japanese proverb

Think of the best class you ever took in high school or college. The teacher was probably clever or used humor along with the class content.

Now think of someone you enjoy being with. Does this person make you laugh? Probably.

Laughter as the best medicine is a serious enough topic to have led Dr. Melissa B. Wanzer, communications professor at Canisius College in Buffalo, New York, to offer a course on the topic, "Constructive Uses of Humor." It's no surprise that this class always fills to capacity. Wanzer's students are required to prepare and perform a stand-up routine in front of the class. They also read journal articles and interpret research studies on humor. In one study, they looked at Southwest Airlines' strategic effort to create a positive environment for employees and customers by integrating humor into the workplace.

Laughter is not just the best thing for improving our general mood; it's also been proven helpful in coping with terminal illness and aging. In her research, Wanzer learned that humor had tremendous benefits for patients and health care providers.

In his now classic book, Norman Cousins (1979) told how he overcame Ankylosing spondylitis, an incurable and fatal spinal column disease, by ignoring his doctors' advice and instead spending a month laughing at his favorite humor and comic books. When Cousins returned to his doctors for a checkup, his disease had disappeared. His book encourages patients to get involved in their own health care and points to the positive effects of humor in curing disease. See http://www.laughingdiva.com/how-laughter-therapy-cured-norman-cousins-of-a-life-threatening-form-of-arthritis/.

While researchers are still debating the physical changes that make laughter beneficial, they all agree that it's good for us.

Fortunately, we don't have to become, or hang out with, stand-up comedians to add more humor to our lives. We can find humor in small things around us. We can even poke fun at ourselves. Because personalities differ, we vary in what we consider funny. Here's a popular joke that will bring a full range of reactions from a smile to a belly laugh.

> A young man asks God how long a million years *is* to him.
>
> God says, "A million years to you is like a single second to me."
>
> "So," says the young man, "what's a million *dollars* to you?"
>
> And God says, "A million dollars to you is like a single penny to me."
>
> And the young man says, "Gee, could I have one of your pennies?"
>
> And God smiles and says, "Certainly. Just wait a second."

Master something and feel good about it

One day, a couple decades ago, I decided I was going to learn to program my VCR. (Look it up if you're under twenty-one.) I sat down with the user's manual and vowed not to get up until I had mastered it. Yippee! I did it!

The bad news about my accomplishment, however, is that as soon as we experience this good-feeling-from-accomplishing-something-technical, some new device comes out, not to mention upgrades to all your current technology, and you get to work up to a new good feeling. Since the day I decided to take over maintaining my websites and set up my own blogs, I have been climbing up steep learning curves. For example, I agreed with my daughter that we should buy appliances with easy-to-master features. When I remodeled my kitchen, that was the primary feature I required—with sturdy and easy to clean next on the list.

I thought I wanted chrome appliances. But when I was in the showroom, I saw how my handprint on the chrome refrigerator door stayed there for all to see. That made "handprint remaining visible on the refrigerator" a new determining factor.

I bought a black refrigerator with a leather-like finish. No handprints.

It's far easier to make wise decisions about buying appliances, of course, than it is to adapt to changes in online technology. Although online technology frequently throws challenges my way, it also provides many opportunities for feel-good experiences when I'm able—on my own—to figure out the latest thing. It also gives me confidence that I'll be able to master the next thing they throw my way.

The thing you choose to master doesn't have to be something big, like figuring out a computer program or learning how to use all the features on your mobile device. For example, I once figured out that an inexpensive clock I loved had stopped working simply because its battery contacts needed to be cleaned and it needed a new battery. It still makes me feel good because I first thought the clock was hopeless and considered throwing it away. Now when I look at it, I beam with pride, knowing I fixed it myself!

Have you ever felt good because you mastered an appliance, gadget, or skill? What was it, and what did you learn?

Practice random acts of kindness

In spite of what we hear on the news and even though it means we'll get taken sometimes, we have to hold onto our belief in the goodness of humankind. Mother Teresa is credited with saying that when we are kind, some people will take advantage of us, but we should be kind anyway.

I was in a fast-food restaurant drive-thru with my grandkids one day. When I rolled up to pay and get our food, the clerk handed me the food and said, "Your food has been paid for by the car that was in front of you."

That was the first time I can remember being the recipient of a random act of kindness. I don't know what motivated that person to pay for our meal, and the car was gone before I could even see who was inside or say thank you. Since then, I have on occasion extended the same kindness to strangers. I have been on both sides of kindness, and it feels good both ways.

WHISTLE WHILE YOU WORK

Enjoy what you do. During college, I worked briefly at a number of jobs to earn money—jobs I knew would never be my career because I didn't love the work and conditions enough. One semester, I worked as a typist for an electronics repair shop. Yes, at one time people got their radios, stereos, etc., repaired instead of throwing them away and buying new ones. My boss was kind enough, and it was mindless work I could easily do, but it was not fulfilling. My boss was sorry to see me leave at the end of the semester. Another year, I worked in the mimeograph department at the university. We provided low-cost printing before photocopying was invented. My job was to type manuscripts for professors onto a stencil. The finished stencil was then wrapped around the drum of a huge mimeograph machine that could print hundreds of handouts for classes or professional presentations. It was gratifying work because I was a fast and accurate typist, but the regimentation was inhuman. Our morning breaks were ten minutes long, and we were even expected to ask permission to go to the restroom.

These experiences were not without their benefits. They renewed my determination to finish college so I could begin my career of choice—teaching. After watching coworkers drag themselves to jobs they didn't enjoy,

I also promised myself that I would never work at something I didn't enjoy, no matter how much it paid.

And furthermore, I insisted on freedom and the flexibility to use my skills to help empower the lives of others. That's exactly what I've done in my career.

Don't get me wrong. I haven't been enthralled with every coworker or supervisor I've had over the years. Plus, there's something to dislike about every job. But I have felt competent and gratified with my work, and I've been rewarded with good pay.

According to a report on MSNBC.com, more than half of American workers are dissatisfied with their jobs. And, contrary to what many may think, it's not just blue collar workers who are unhappy. After starting their careers, many doctors, dentists, and lawyers discover they don't enjoy their work. Some confess to yielding to family or social pressure to seek these "prestigious" or "family tradition" careers, but once they begin doing the work, they feel pressured to stay, largely because of the need to repay their exorbitant student loans.

Complaining about work is a favorite lunchtime topic for many employees. For some, it's the highlight of the workday.

Why would we stay in a job we hate? We need to earn money, most people say, to feed our families and pay our bills. You'll get no argument about that. But couldn't we do that just as well, perhaps even better, working at something we love?

Not according to some job-haters. These are workers

who feel stuck, defeated, and incapable of changing their lives. They expend precious hours of their lives tolerating uninteresting work and feeling antagonistic toward their coworkers and emotionally abusive bosses. They show up day after day, week after week, year after year in exchange for money that, in some cases, barely pays their bills.

Then there are the folks looking for easy money. They're not unlike petty thieves. They stay at jobs they hate, knowing they'll get paid even if they do the minimum or less. These employees enjoy defrauding the company by clocking out late but leaving early, taking three-hour lunch breaks, and leaving the bulk of work to other employees who have a higher sense of responsibility. These dishonest employees actually feel empowered by their deceit.

Another type of employee has such low self-esteem and self-confidence that she stays on a job she hates because she doesn't believe she can get another one. These folks are like abused spouses who stay with their partners, believing, among other flawed beliefs, that they will never find—or don't deserve—another, better partner.

And of course there are the professionals mentioned above who exchange position and prestige for money but give poor service to their patients and clients.

Wouldn't it be great if what we love to do and what we get paid for were the same job?

Such work may sound magical, mysterious, or out of reach, but it isn't. It does, however, take courage to look for it. And do it. For this concept to work, you must discover what you really enjoy doing. Your first thought may be that you'd enjoy doing nothing. I'm sure you would indeed enjoy that… for a little while. But soon you'd get bored and your human spirit would long for meaningful activity, for something to do.

During a retreat I once attended, we were asked to visualize our ideal day. After taking a few minutes to capture this dream day in our minds, we shared it with the group. Many of us visualized ourselves living in houses on the beach, being pampered by servants, and making mad, passionate love to "Pablo" or "Desiree."

There was one common element in each person's ideal day. We all visualized doing some type of job, having a career, or owning our own business. My ideal day included overseeing an ample office located in my spacious home and staffed by ten assistants who helped manage my itinerary, speaking engagements, book signings, and other important tasks required to properly keep my empire going.

Not one of us visualized an ideal day as one where we did nothing all day.

We are all drawn to work. Having work to do gives our lives structure. If we love what we do, the work also gives our lives meaning. Your job is more than what you do to make money. It's a big chunk of your life. It should be your mission. If it doesn't feel that way to you, it isn't too late for you to make a better choice about your work. Commit to finding work you love and reap the joy of getting paid to do it. That way, your "happy hour" will not be after work, from five to six in the evening. It will be from nine to five! You may even whistle while you work.

AIM FOR AN ORDINARY DAY

People frequently say, "Have an extraordinary day." What does that say about an ordinary day?

In our haste to attain exceptional success, fantastic relationships, and exorbitant amounts of money, many of us miss out on the beauty of the ordinary day. Neill (2007) shared about the time his friend and mentor Steve Chandler said to him, "Have an average day!"

Neill was surprised by this until Chandler explained what was behind it. Chandler explained that one of his mentors, Lyndon Duke, had studied the linguistics of suicide. After studying suicide notes, Duke determined that the enemy of happiness is "the curse of exceptionality." You see, he reasoned, if everyone was exceptional, then being exceptional would become commonplace. In this case, since exceptional means standing out from the rest, everyone would fail.

And, as anyone who has excelled knows, being exceptional can bring on feelings of isolation, estrangement, and anxiety. On the other hand, believing you can never attain greatness can make you believe your life is worthless and without meaning.

When Duke was struggling with his own unhappiness, he noticed one day that his neighbor was singing as he mowed the lawn. Duke had an aha! moment. He suddenly realized that appreciation for simple everyday pleasures was what was absent from his life.

Give meaning to your life by making small differences every day. Smile at a stranger, say a kind word to a friend, spend time with your children and loved ones. Be an average, happy person making a small positive difference, and having a happy, average day. In doing this, you create a kind of exceptionality that everyone can share. Smile more often.

Are you aware that people can hear you smile on the telephone? Smiling is also one of the quickest ways to lift your mood.

During decades of research, Ekman, Davidson, and Friesen (1990) reported a full smile that involves your eyes and your mouth can lift your mood and reduce your stress. Even faking a smile, according to Pressman and Kraft (2012), can lift your mood. More than just your mood, Iacoboni (2009) found that a smile is contagious and even uplifts the moods of those around you.

Shake your booty

You don't need to go out or have a date to do this one. Never mind that you can't qualify for *So You Think You Can Dance,* the American televised dance competition that began in 2005. Just turn on some music and dance around your house! There's no wrong way to get going, and you don't even have to be any good at it.

Want more structure? Find a YouTube video or DVD that suits your style. Whether it's hip-hop, ballet, zumba, line dancing, ballroom, or salsa, get busy moving your body. The activity will lower your anxiety, lift your mood, and maybe even shrink that booty.

> Color your life *harmonious* by adding some green—plants or a garden view—to your décor, no matter what your color scheme. Green is the second most popular color after blue. Green helps alleviate anxiety and promote harmony.

Cry when you feel like it

When you feel like crying, let the tears flow. Crying is not necessarily an indication of sadness. We cry for emotional release, sometimes after a stressful or painful situation has been resolved. Other times, we cry following a loss like the death of a loved one. This healthy type of crying is important for self-nurturing. We even cry when we're very happy about an outcome. Many happiness seekers think being happy means you're never sad. That couldn't be further from the truth.

Some years ago, about four hours before leaving for a night at the theater, I learned that my sister had been diagnosed with breast cancer and that another relative had been arrested and accused of a horrific crime. I let the tears flow and flow.

Because I was always taught when I was young that "big girls don't cry," it isn't always easy for me to cry today.

But I've experienced the cleansing effect of crying. I'm convinced that holding sadness inside—trying hard not to cry—is harmful to our health. The best way to be happy is to cry when you need to. Once the painful experience is gone and your emotional release has taken place, your inner joy has the space to return. This is because your inner joy is not really tied to outside events. You just think it is.

Be still and breathe

When I was still teaching full time, I had adventures with the photocopier. Every now and then, the copier in our campus workroom stopped working. There were no indicator lights that told us to call for repair. It didn't need toner. It didn't seem to be overheating. Then, usually after about an hour, the copier started to run well again.

My theory is that the machine just needed a break from nonstop copying. Since we wouldn't willingly give it a break, however, it took its own breaks. We need to do that, too. Most advice on finding happiness suggests breathing deeply, being still, meditating, and praying.

Value yourself

> *Until you value yourself, you will not value your time. Until you value your time, you will not do anything with it.*
>
> —M. Scott Peck

If you were raised as I was to be unselfish, modest, and perhaps even self-effacing, you were misled. If we are to have the love and respect of others, we must learn to love and respect ourselves. Loving yourself does not mean being narcissistic, selfish, manipulative, or mean. Folks with these characteristics don't love themselves at all. They're seeking validation from the outside. When they don't get it, they lash out in mean and sometimes violent ways. The self-love I'm suggesting means recognizing that you are a whole and perfect child of the universe and that you have much of value to share with the world.

Do you love and value yourself? Try this. Step up to the mirror, look at your beautiful self and say, "I love you." If you've never done this before, you'll probably feel very strange, maybe even uncomfortable, talking to yourself in the mirror. You may not even believe yourself at first. Until you can do this mirror exercise and feel good about it, just say, "I love you!" to yourself throughout the day. Try it. Not only will you feel better, but you'll also attract good things into your life.

Try something new

Challenge yourself. Your challenge might be training for a marathon. It might be as simple as taking a different route home from work or school, trying a new recipe, or learning a new computer program. Research on preventing Alzheimer's reports the tremendous benefits to the brain that challenging ourselves and trying new activities give us. The Internet is loaded with new ideas and with lots of free tutorials.

I began learning Spanish using a free Internet program, https://www.Duolingo.com. The lessons are presented in small segments with plenty of interactive practice. You can compete with friends if you wish or join a discussion board to review what you're learning. If you feel inclined, you can also jump to the Immersion tab and go straight into reading whole articles in Spanish, German, French, Portuguese, or Italian.

Be here and now

My family and I attended the retirement ceremony of one of my nephews, who had served twenty years in the Navy. While enjoying the delicious food and hospitality on his patio, I asked my daughter, "How do we get back to the freeway from here?" The reception had barely begun, and here I was, already racing into the future, thinking about our route home. Fortunately, my daughter chided me. "Mom," she said, "be here and now." I snapped back and engaged in conversation, and enjoyed the beauty of my surroundings.

Be kind to others and yourself. Jumping out of bed and being spectacular every day is not necessary for happiness. There are times when you may feel like staying in bed longer to rest and reflect. Give yourself permission to lounge around or do what you want, not what you think you should. If there are tasks that just must be done on a given day, do them quickly and treat yourself afterwards.

Other ways to take care of yourself

- Avoid taking on more than you can handle.
- Schedule breaks in your day and in your week.
- Take pride in your achievements, but give yourself a break when you make a mistake.
- Pamper yourself on occasion.
- Eat nourishing food that enhances your energy and spirit.
- Always breathe deeply.
- Get adequate sustained sleep, even if it requires investing in a new mattress or pillows.

Make change as easy as possible

When we set out to make changes, we often set ourselves up for failure by taking on too much or setting insurmountable goals. Let's say you decide you want to increase your physical exercise. It would be a big mistake to set the goal of running three miles a day if you've been sedentary up to now. It won't take you long to stumble, run out of breath, get discouraged, and give up. How do we make change easier?

One easy-to do-technique is *kaizen*, the Japanese art of relatively small, continuous improvements. *Kaizen* works by pairing the new behavior with a habit you already have and keeping the change so small that you can't fail. If you want to begin a walking regimen, for example, put on your tennis shoes as soon as you take off your pajamas. Then, for starters, walk to the mailbox and back. Once this new behavior is a habit, expand a little. Walk to the end of the block and back. Be sure your new behavior is such a small step that you can't fail. Get more ideas from Nicholas Ritchey's (2012) blog post, "Kaizen: Accomplishing Big Goals with Tiny Steps."

More ways to simplify your life

- Resign from commitments you're not passionate about.
- Get up on the other side of the bed or make some other small change in your routine.
- Drop subscriptions to newsletters and magazines you no longer want to read.
- Devote at least one hour a day to doing something you really enjoy.
- Get caller ID on your telephone and answer only the calls you want to answer.
- Turn off the ringer and let voice mail answer your phone when you want to rest.
- Automate regular activities, such as paying bills, watering the lawn, etc.
- Keep up with your car's maintenance schedule.
- Spend some part of your day in quiet prayer or meditation.
- Cook several meals at once so you can have a week free of daily cooking.
- Learn to ask for and accept help.
- Clear away the clutter.
- Little by little, pay off credit card debt and begin paying with cash.
- Stop trying to be perfect!

Another technique was presented by Ashley Davis Bush (2011), a licensed psychotherapist and grief counselor, who asserted that when we seek to change, we are asking our brain to form new grooves, which requires repetition of the new behavior. For this to work, we need a trigger, something that reminds us to do the new response. Bush offered tips in the form of triggers and tools. For example:

> *Trigger:* Coming home at the end of a stressful day
>
> *Tool:* Before you enter your house, shake down your body as if shaking off water. Shake one foot and leg, then the other. Shake your arms and hands. Then gently shake your head, relax your shoulders, and take a deep breath and let out a prolonged sigh.

Summary

So there you have it. Success and wealth don't lead to happiness. It's the other way around: Happiness leads to your success and wealth, in whatever way you define these. So it's worthwhile to choose happiness. How about you? What's your recipe for happiness?

People who describe themselves as happy often live a simple life. This doesn't mean they don't enjoy some of the conveniences that modern life offers. They just don't tie their well-being to things outside themselves.

You can live a happier life by slowing down to enjoy the food and comforts you have. You can prevent adversities from overtaking you by repeating a favorite scripture or affirmation or by laughing more often. Instead of shunning work, insist on having a job or career that you enjoy. Challenge yourself to master something you bought but don't know how to use. Try something new that you've thought about but never done.

Be kind to yourself by treating yourself well and surrounding yourself with positive people who inspire, encourage, and celebrate you. Keep your focus on the here and now so you can enjoy all those things and people that surround you. Give yourself permission to laugh, cry, dance, and be still. Finally, automate things that don't need the human touch and save your time and energy for those things that do.

When you're kind to yourself, this kindness increases your energy, improves your attitude, and makes you more compassionate toward others. It will, in fact, be easy to be kind to others, for you will be putting a variation of the Golden Rule into effect. You're "doing unto them as you would have done unto yourself."

HAPPINESS FLASHBACK

I often sang Brahms' Lullaby to lull my babies to sleep. When my second daughter, Sonya, was just a few months old, she had only to hear me sing the first line before she would close her eyes and begin to hum the rest of the lullaby on her own until she finally hummed herself to sleep. It was amazing.

Harmonizing Family and Work

You don't choose your family. They are God's gift to you, as you are to them.

—Desmond Tutu

When I see parents pushing a baby in a stroller, I often wonder if they realize what a precious life they have been given. And more, I wonder if they realize what a tremendous opportunity they have to help this new life grow up to be a joyful, happy, and loving person.

So many of us get caught up earning the money we need to take care of our families that we neglect to devote the time, love, and energy to them that they deserve.

Even as a very young girl, I always expected to have both a family and a career. None of that either/or stuff for me. Growing up watching my mother run a successful home-based beauty shop while she raised three girls probably had something to do with my ambitions. Seeing her play the piano and organ at our church every Sunday, then dash home to cook a scrumptious dinner convinced me that balance was quite doable. I didn't learn until later that this harmonizing act required skill, determination, and a secret ingredient.

The secret to harmonizing your family and career is learning to take care of yourself first.

Wait! Don't panic. I don't mean you should neglect either your family or ignore your business. I mean you should do the things that make you happy and are important to you, so you feel full. By full, I mean complete, believing that you are enough. When you're not engaged in satisfying activities, a career you love, and fulfilling your life's purpose, you will feel an emptiness. Some people try to fill this emptiness with external pleasures like food, drink, drugs, sex, and other risky behavior. Those don't work. Only by taking care of your needs and pursuing the life you love will you be able to give to your family and others.

Think about this. When airline attendants go through the emergency information just before the plane takes off, they always say, "In the unlikely event of loss of air pressure in the cabin, an oxygen mask will drop down. Put the oxygen mask on yourself first before assisting a child traveling with you." In other words, you won't be able to help anyone else if you're incapacitated. The same thing is true in the rest of your life.

This simple truth applies especially when it comes to

harmonizing your family and your career. You must take care of your own physical, psychological, emotional, and spiritual health so you'll be able to work and be there for your family.

But there's another important reason you should take care of yourself first. Your children, partner, family, customers, and others learn how to treat you based on the way you treat yourself. If you value, honor, and respect yourself, then others will, too.

MAKE HARMONIZING FAMILY AND WORK A TOP PRIORITY IN YOUR LIFE

Until recent years, it was mainly women (but not men) who faced the challenge of harmonizing family and work. That's because, despite all our modern thinking and open lifestyles, the woman is still expected to bear the major responsibility for maintaining the family and the household—even if she's a corporate CEO or the first woman elected president of a country. Advice on harmonizing family and work is still addressed to women in publications like *Parents Magazine*, websites like *Working Mother*, and increasingly in business publications like *Forbes*. Fair (2013) breathes fresh air into the parenting advice arena by confessing that it's impossible to perfectly balance the ups and downs of juggling family and career. Her guilt-free tips urge us not to aim for perfection, but to decide what matters most and is long-lasting for our children, caring for ourselves, and enjoying satisfying careers too.

There's no question that both family and work are important. Without income from work, the family cannot be housed and fed. But without a harmonious family, the benefits of work are lost. It is the responsibility of *both* parents, whether one or both have outside jobs, run a business, or stay at home.

Creating harmony is critical to family happiness. We need only to look at the lives of successful celebrity parents to see the struggles and failures disharmony can cause. Perhaps one of the most notable examples of inharmonious parenting was Bing Crosby, famous for his crooning love songs and his smooth rendition of "White Christmas." As friendly and easy-going as he was on the screen, he was known by friends and others to be a violent, neglectful, and abusive parent to his four sons from his first marriage. After Bing's death, his oldest son, Gary, wrote a tell-all book, *Going My Own Way*, about the abuse and neglect he and his brothers suffered. Sometime after the book's publication, Gary confessed that he exaggerated some of his claims. Two of Gary's brothers committed suicide and the third one died of a heart attack. Bing Crosby was loved by his fans for the gentle, loving, and happy-go-lucky guy he seemed to be in his songs and movies, but in his most important role—parenting—all the benefits of his fame and wealth seemed lost, at least with his first family.

In his second marriage, Bing was older and spent more time with the children of this marriage. Thus, they remember him with much love and affection. The PBS documentary *Bing Crosby Rediscovered* neither vilifies Bing nor puts him on a pedestal.

Another celebrity parent, Joan Crawford, was the main character in another famous tell-all book, *Mommie Dearest*, written in 1978 by her adopted daughter, Christina Crawford, and made into a movie in 1981. According to Christina and her brother, Christopher, Joan Crawford's bouts with alcohol and men and the stress of her acting career caused her to become abusive. Joan's obsession with perfection made life unbearable for Christina and her brother as they found they couldn't live up to their mother's standards.

While there is much we adults can do to help ourselves overcome sad, abusive, and horrible childhoods, it would clearly be far better to have been nurtured and valued in a loving environment as children. We can do for our children what our parents did not do for us. We can maintain a harmonious family and succeed in a career. This is the toughest harmonizing act in life, and yet many achieve it. How do they do it? Most important, *how can you do it?*

I've already mentioned the importance of taking care of yourself first. What else can you do to ensure that you will be able to harmonize family and career?

Start with intention

I've always marveled at the way a cocktail waitress correctly remembers the drink order of each person in a large group without writing it down. When she returns to the table later, she asks who wants a refill, again remembering the drink order of each person. Most amazing is when the party leaves and a new group is seated at the same table, the process starts again. The waitress erases the previous group's orders from her mental slate and now takes the new drink orders. How is she able to do that? Intention. She plans to remember, has faith that she will remember, and commits to remembering.

To harmonize family and work, you must intend to do so and commit to it. Decide that you want harmony, then be willing to do whatever it takes to bring it about. You can't approach raising a family and succeeding at work as a "maybe" or a test run. It isn't a rehearsal. It's your life, and you must live it full speed ahead if it is to be harmonized and happy.

Give up the *if-onlys* and *what-ifs*.

Looking at the present as a reason for not going after what you want is a trap. It holds you back from finding ways to get what you want.

If only I had sent my children to private school, they would have gotten better jobs.

A person who looks backwards is like someone driving forward while looking in the rearview mirror. You are focusing on something you can't change while ignoring the only time you can change: the here and now.

If you do find regrets of past actions creeping into your mind today, use those regrets as lessons to help you create a better life now. But also use them to forgive yourself and others. Here's how:

1. *Accept responsibility for the mistake you believe you made, but don't dwell on it.* A problem claimed is a problem that can be reframed. I like to ask myself, "What did I learn from the experience?" as a way to begin healing.
2. *Give yourself credit for being a caring person.* If you didn't care, you wouldn't feel guilt, shame, or pain for your behavior. Use your past behavior only as a starting point to build a different future.
3. *Don't waste time thinking that forgiveness means condoning mistakes or poor judgment.* You're human and therefore guaranteed to make errors. Forgive yourself so you can heal.
4. *Imagine what you would say to your best friend if she were in the same situation.* Chances are, you would offer her encouragement. Say these words of encouragement to yourself.
5. *Think of one small step forward you can take.* Once you can take one small step forward, you are no longer stuck. Now you are in transition, which is a great place to be.
6. *Look around you and think about the things in your life you have to be grateful for.* Dwell on the fact that there are many in the world who would consider themselves wealthy to have some of the things, relationships, and experiences you take for granted.
7. *If your regrets linger, get professional help from a therapist, group, spiritual leader, or medical professional. There's no need to go it alone.*

The idea is to *work with what you have*. You don't need a mansion, and you don't need to shower your family with toys and gifts to be happy and successful. Your *intention* to create harmony in your family is the best start.

Make a lifelong commitment

Once your consciousness has formed your intention, then you must commit to it. When you welcome a new child into your family, for example, it must be with absolute certainty that this child has a permanent and special place in your life. It's easy to see the weakness of a half commitment, as in "I'll try raising you and see how it works out." It can only lead to a halfhearted attempt at parenting. When you've committed to your marriage and family, everything else you do gets blended in.

Here's an example from when my children were young and taking music lessons. Many parents think of lessons as an opportunity to send their children off somewhere to learn to play an instrument, but we chose a method that involved a deep family commitment, not just dropping them off at lessons once every other week.

I expected my children to take piano lessons because my mother, a pianist and organist, required piano lessons of my siblings and me. But when I was a parent and a coworker told me about a unique violin program, I was fascinated, especially when I learned that very young children can take lessons.

My oldest daughter was just two and a half years old when her teacher, Dorée Huneven, returned from Japan after being trained in the Suzuki Method. Dorée was hired by the School of Performing Arts at the University of Southern California. My daughter was one of eight or nine youngsters who became her first students. They studied the Suzuki Method, created by Dr. Shinichi Suzuki, whose father owned a violin factory in Japan and expected his son to take over the business. Instead, after being inspired by hearing Ukrainian violinist Mischa Elman play Schubert's "Ave Maria," Suzuki taught himself to play the violin. After perfecting his own playing with the help of several great teachers, he and his brothers formed a string quartet. It was during a rehearsal with his brothers in 1933 that an idea struck Suzuki. After observing that all Japanese children grew up speaking Japanese, he realized that children could learn music or anything else the same way they learn language. This came to be called the "mother tongue method." Because the violin was his instrument, he began to apply this theory to violin instruction. Suzuki also strongly believed that every child has the potential to be great if nurtured in a caring environment.

As soon as we enrolled our children in Suzuki violin lessons, we received a record (later a tape) of compositions from the first book with instructions to listen to it every day, not in formal sit-down sessions, but as part of our regular day. We put the record on first thing in the morning as we got ready for work and school. By the time our second child was born, playing the Suzuki record every morning had become such a routine in our household that my husband continued to put it on every morning when my oldest daughter and I were away for a week attending a music workshop. He didn't even realize he'd been doing it until we returned. We had a good laugh about the force of habit.

Suzuki believed that by hearing the repertoire daily, children would become so familiar with it that by the time they learned to play each piece, they would aim to match their technique and tone to what they had heard so many times—the way we learn language. As my daughter listened to the repertoire every day, we all listened with her. Our involvement with the violin extended beyond lessons. We attended many related activities—group rehearsals, workshops, and recitals—with other students and their parents.

We also scheduled parties with the other parents to celebrate each book's completion and our children's progress. One father created a cake shaped like a violin for his child's party. Because my daughter learned to play Bach's minuets before she could read the music, I created lyrics to Minuets 1 and 2 (so named in the Suzuki repertoire) to make it easy for her to practice certain passages. For our family and many others, the Suzuki Method was more than just violin lessons; it was a way of life. If you wish, you can see and even sing the lyrics at http://coloryourlifehappy.com/bach-minuets.

Be part of your children's lives

Nature always wears the colors of the spirit.
—Ralph Waldo Emerson

Get involved with the many aspects of your children's lives. My youngest daughter and I attended a follow-up meeting at a local church after she'd attended a youth retreat. The leader asked questions to see how well we parents knew our children. Many parents didn't know their child's favorite color, movie, or singer. I was surprised and relieved when I passed the pop quiz.

As children approach puberty, they may outwardly appear to resent your involvement, but inwardly they appreciate and crave it. By involvement, of course, I don't mean harassing them, hounding them, or invading their privacy.

Be involved with their activities. It's especially important to attend their sports, music, and after-school activities. Take them to the movies they want to see, read the books they read, and listen to the music they listen to—no matter how hard listening is! When I have trouble understanding the lyrics to the songs my children and grandchildren listen to, I look them up on the Internet. Yikes! Some of it is pretty racy by baby-boomer standards, but you need to know what's getting into their minds.

Don't make the mistake I made in my early days of parenting: Don't voice your shock and resentment loudly and angrily. That just seems to push them toward the subject of your ire. Some parents ban all rap and hip-hop music from their homes, but you can't ban it from the world. As soon as your child leaves your home, the music you may find objectionable surrounds them. Trying to stop it is like trying to stop the sunshine. It's better to be aware of what your children listen to so you can offer alternative messages.

I enjoyed reading the books my children were reading and helping them with book reports. Honestly, though, because I enjoy research and writing, I was more excited about their book reports than they were. My husband always cringed when he heard one of the kids announce, "I have to do a book report," because he knew there would be loud disagreements and arguments, and tempers would flare before the report was in its final form.

Helping your children with homework is a good time to mention that giving up on perfection is your best strategy (more about this later). Walking that line between guiding your children and allowing them to find their own way can be treacherous. At times, you will feel you've been too heavy-handed, whereas at other times, you may feel as though you've surrendered to a better-armed enemy.

There will also be times when you're going to have to participate in activities you don't like. Even though I'm not a fan of animated movies, for example, I sat through countless numbers of them with my children and grandchildren... just trying to stay awake. Fortunately, when I did fall asleep, the crescendos of the closing music woke me up so I could comment on how interesting the movie had been. But it didn't work. Kids are too smart to be fooled by this tactic. They learned to be content with my physical presence, if not my full attention in movies.

One day, my grandsons tried, without success, to teach me how to avoid being shot down in one of those action video games. I was amazed at how skillful they were; they were appalled at how terrible I was and thought my failed attempts were hilarious.

Create a spiritual partnership

We usually need help to successfully harmonize our family and career. The saying "It takes a village to raise a child" alludes to the part others play in creating that harmony. The most important partnership is with your spiritual source. I'm not speaking of religion, but a belief in something greater than or outside yourself. And I'm making that distinction between religion and spirituality for a good reason.

Religion, ideally the source of comfort that provides moral guidelines for like-minded people, has throughout history and even today been tied to wars, violence, discrimination, pain, and suffering. Many people have lost faith in traditional religions, which do not provide the unconditional love, acceptance, and peace they seek. While any given religion is based on a set of stories, rituals, and conclusions created by its founders, spirituality is a personal belief in a higher power without the dogma. Religions, thanks to their commitment to incontrovertible beliefs, promote separation. Spirituality, by respecting the individual's right to choose from a wide spectrum of beliefs, promotes inclusion. Your spiritual life is the thread that holds all other aspects of your life together. It doesn't matter what names you assign to your spiritual source—what's important is that you connect with it.

No one has trouble understanding that we need to fill our gas tanks regularly if we want our vehicles to run. Nor do we have difficulty understanding the need to eat every day, even if we ate three full meals the day before. Connecting with your spiritual source every day keeps your life and that of your family harmonized in ways far more important than the worldly habits of eating or filling our cars with gas. Your spiritual source is like a GPS that helps you navigate through life and stay on track as you move toward your goals.

A spiritual source can also provide solace when you are stressed or comfort when you are grieving.

How does spirituality connect with happiness?

Results of a study by Holder, Coleman, and Wallace (2010) revealed that spirituality is one key to children's happiness. They asked 320 children, ages eight to twelve, to complete six questionnaires to rate their happiness, spirituality, religiousness, and temperament. The children were from four public schools and two faith-based schools. Their parents were also asked to rate the happiness and temperaments of their children.

Children found to be the happiest had an inner belief

system by which they saw their lives as having value and meaning. They also had deep, high-quality relationships. These are thought to be key features of spirituality.

Spirituality is not tied to church attendance or religious instruction. Since personal meaning and relationships with others have been strongly associated with happiness, the researchers recommend enhancing spirituality in children.

Since other research has shown that expressing kindness and helping others also enhance personal meaning and increase happiness, parents are encouraged to promote these qualities and habits in their children.

Although research on children's happiness is rare, the findings of this study parallel what has been found in countless studies of happiness in adults: Happiness is tied to spiritual meaning and positive relationships with others. If these studies are right, then those of us seeking happiness must connect to our own spirituality.

The paths to spirituality share common themes:

- Believing in a higher power, no matter what name you give it
- Finding strength and comfort as a result of tapping into this power
- Being able to feel surrounded and filled by this power
- Believing that you and all other people are an expression of this power
- Feeling a connection to other people, nature, and the universe

Getting in touch with your spirituality doesn't require that you subscribe to any specific, organized religion or belief system. Although many people enjoy gathering at religious services with others who share their beliefs, this is not a requirement. Finding your own spiritual path, however, is critical to your happiness and peace of mind.

Six ways to access your spiritual path

1. ***Listen to your inner voice.*** Sometimes we call this intuition. It requires you to get still and listen to your own inner voice. You don't have to be religious or at prayer to do this. Most of us have had the sense of an inner self at some time. Taking time from the flurry of daily activities to be still is comforting and replenishing.

Quieting your thoughts and meditating is the simplest way to get started. If you've never tried to sit still for a few minutes without thinking of anything, you'll be surprised at how challenging it is at first. It takes practice to accomplish stillness. But it's worth the practice because you'll find that meditating can be very beneficial.

Begin small, just one minute a day, and increase the time little by little. As you practice, listen to messages and thoughts that come up as a result.

Prayer works for people around the world. Some pray to the deity of their religion; others pray to the universe, the universal mind, or a higher power. Tapping your spiritual source is powerful because you're acknowledging the fact that there is a power greater than you in this universe.

You're recognizing your connection to it and accessing the benefits it provides.

2. ***Commune with nature.*** You may find your spiritual path by communing with nature on walks, growing a garden, studying the constellation and stars, or attending retreats in remote locations. One author created a sanctuary in his backyard where he could go to be still and meditate, but you don't have to build anything if you don't want to. Many manmade and natural sanctuaries already exist for your use.

When we took our four children for a week in Yosemite Park, for example, we were unprepared for its awesome size and beauty. We opted to stay in what was called a tent cabin. It had solid walls, a canvas roof, and a rustic outdoor kitchen. There were electrical outlets in the wooden work area, but we didn't know that before we left home, so we cooked everything over a fire we made each day.

Our tent cabin was near a river and only a few steps from the common restrooms, and there was also an attached laundry area where we could also wash our dishes. I never saw the children so happy washing dishes, probably because it involved a short trek, crunching on the uneven ground leading to the laundry area.

During the day, we visited majestic waterfalls and explored steep forest trails. At night, we cooked hot dogs and toasted marshmallows over a campfire. Being out in nature and away from our usual activities, we slowed down our lives, became closer as a family, and discovered the peace and rejuvenation that only nature can provide. We didn't want to leave. It was one of the best vacations we ever had.

Even if you don't believe in a higher power, you can find tremendous peace, joy, and inspiration being outdoors and enjoying nature's sounds, smells, and sights. You gain a new perspective and a respect for the here and now.

Kaplan and Kaplan (1989) discovered that engaging with natural environments increases our ability to focus. Their work, which they called Attention Restoration Theory, uncovered that activities such as walking through a park or arboretum could diminish such stress as road rage and bolster our spirits.

Rudd, Aaker, and Vohs (2012) discovered that when their subjects experienced the awe-inspiring beauty and peace of amazing sites like Yosemite, the breathtaking scope of the Grand Canyon, or the ethereal beauty of the Aurora Borealis, they felt like they had more time and were more patient, less materialistic, and more willing to volunteer time to help others.

3. *Move your body.* Dancing has been a traditional part of religious and spiritual services for a long time. In the Bible, dance is often described as a way to express joy: *Let them praise his name with dancing and make music to him with timbrel and harp* (Psalms 149:3 and 150:4 NIV). When I was a teen, I performed an interpretive dance at my church while reciting "The Creation" by James Weldon Johnson. I wore a white flowing robe-like costume.

The musician played a piece that matched the drama of the poem. It was a stirring performance for both me and the audience.

Gabrielle Roth (2011), a dancer and musician, saw dance in a bigger and deeper way. She wrote that dance is

> the fastest, most direct route to the truth— not some big truth that belongs to everybody, but the get down and personal kind, the what's-happening-in-me-right-now kind of truth. We dance to reclaim our brilliant ability to disappear in something bigger, something safe, a space without a critic or a judge or an analyst.

Roth founded 5Rhythms, a school of experimental theater, and although she died in 2012, her work continues at http://www.gabrielleroth.com/. You can see dances she created on YouTube and learn how to perform them yourself.

4. ***Connect with other people and pets, too.*** After finishing a treatment, an acupuncturist asked the patient if he was lonely. Surprised at the question, the patient said of course he had loads of friends and acquaintances. But then she asked how often he spent time with them face to face. How often we equate knowing lots of people with having friends. The acupuncturist pointed out that he sensed in this patient a loss of connection that only close relationships and quality time with people we care about can fill.

We are born alone but are hardwired to thrive, thanks to positive connections with others. Whether we are socializing, helping those less fortunate, spending precious time with family and friends, or showing kindness to a complete stranger, social connections enrich us and create well-being. Allen R. McConnell and colleagues (2011) found in a study that pet owners enjoyed the well-being and support they received from pets and that this connection complemented rather than competed with human contacts.

When we think of making connections, we don't always think of pets, but animals are another source of social support and unconditional love. According to the American Humane Society, nearly half of U.S. households have at least one dog. About one fourth of those who have dogs have two. According to pet-ownership estimates from the American Pet Products Association for 2012, cats are now more popular as pets. There are many other pets that families consider part of the family. Even though I'm one of the few people in my neighborhood without a pet, I can attest to the love my neighbors have for their furry family members.

5. *Enjoy making or appreciating art, music, and literature.* Music is called the universal language because it has the power to speak to all of us—regardless of where we live or what language we speak. It can lift us to unheard-of heights. Some say music is the only language that can reach traumatized and brain-damaged people. Beautiful music seems to flow through the fingers of a skilled pianist or other musician out into the instrument, creating visceral excitement. Music can calm us, bring us to tears, or build bridges across nations and peoples.

Art can also make our lives better. Michelangelo's passion for creating sculpture was deep and profound. He saw himself not as creating art, but rather as releasing a human form trapped in the marble. His famous David, which was created in 1501 when Michelangelo was only twenty-six, still has the power to mesmerize those fortunate enough to view it in person.

Engaging with literature through fiction, nonfiction, and poetry puts us in touch with a part of ourselves we often can't reach in any other way. Learning to read stimulated my imagination as a child and opened up a world beyond my neighborhood and my everyday experiences. My desire to travel was born when I read about other people and their lifestyles and first saw photos of the wonders of the world. Getting lost in simple mysteries such as those written by Helen Fuller Orton, where lost treasures were solved without murder or guns, began my lifelong love of mysteries.

One year, decades ago, I gave my niece Mimi the book *Are You There God? It's Me, Margaret* by Judy Blume. Mimi was twelve at the time, and just like the characters in the book, was perplexed by training bras, kissing boys, and periods. Like Margaret, she could talk to God about it. She tells me that this book was special to her, not just because it was the first book anyone had ever given her with a message to her written inside it, but because the characters were like her. She finished the whole book that first night and read it many times, even into adulthood.

6. ***Connect to God, a higher power, or other deity.*** Many choose this spiritual path, though others say this path chooses them. Spirituality leads to and is a another source of happiness.

My husband, children and I were connected with our spiritual source when we prayed together at meals and at bedtime and engaged in activities at our church. Not only did we attend weekly services, but we also participated in youth groups, summer programs, and music performances. These activities may not be your preferred way to connect with your higher power, however, so I encourage you to find your own way.

Once you're in tune with your spiritual path, you'll discover it's not just a ritual; it's a welcome part of your everyday life. Spirituality also helps with everyday challenges. When I was in the last stages of pregnancy with my fourth child, I was huge, and yet I was still running errands, usually with the other three kids in tow. I was always looking for a parking spot that was as close as possible to the store entrance. I'm not sure who started it, but we got in the habit of reciting the 23rd Psalm to help Mommy find a close parking space. And it worked. Even if the parking lot was full, a car would pull out just as I pulled up and I'd get my ideal parking spot.

Years later, I noticed my fourth child, a preteen at the time, had a hanger in her closet that was empty except for the note folded on it that said "black pants."

"What's this?" I asked her.

"Oh, our teacher at church said that if we believe we will receive," she said, "so I'm believing that the black pants I want are already on the hanger."

Find your own spiritual path by determining what feels right to you. Be grateful for your uniqueness and your experiences, since there is no one path or one right way. Please also know that following your spiritual path will not protect you from things that go wrong in your life, however; pain and suffering are part of the journey. A spiritual path can be your route through the pain, uncertainty, and suffering to get you to your happiness set point.

Make family your highest priority

Once you're committed and in tune with your spiritual source, you will attract into your life many things, people, and circumstances that will manifest your intention.

When my husband and I were raising our children, for example, their concerns and needs were at the center of our planning. When we remodeled our kitchen, I wanted a work island, even though (according to the designer) our kitchen wasn't quite big enough. But the designer was just designing a meal preparation and eating center. I was designing a homework and project center. With my encouragement, the designer found a way to make the work island fit. During the week, it was a wonderful spot for all four children to gather and complete their homework and craft projects. On weekends, it became the family cooking center.

After church on Sundays, we experimented with new recipes I found in newspapers and magazines. Each child helped with chopping, grating, measuring, and pouring. One of those recipes was such a hit with us that decades later, it is still our favorite dish. Every time I serve it, our guests ask for the recipe. Your family may enjoy it as well.

California Zucchini Bake

1 pound lean ground beef or turkey
3 medium zucchini, thinly sliced
¼ cup sliced green onion with tops
2 teaspoons salt
¼ teaspoon garlic powder
2 teaspoons chili powder
1 (7 ounce) can medium hot green chiles, chopped
3 cups cooked rice
1 cup sour cream
2 cups shredded Monterey Jack cheese
4 medium tomatoes, thinly sliced
paprika

Sauté the meat, zucchini, onion, salt, garlic powder, and chili powder in a lightly greased skillet. Stir frequently until meat is no longer pink and zucchini and onions are tender. Stir in the green chiles, rice, sour cream and ½ (1 cup) of the cheese just until well mixed. Remove from heat. Turn into a buttered 9" x 13" casserole dish. Arrange tomato slices in rows on top until the casserole is fully covered. This way, every serving will have a tomato slice. Season with salt and pepper to taste. Top with remaining grated Monterey Jack cheese. Lightly sprinkle paprika on top to add coloring. Bake at 350 degrees for 20 to 25 minutes or until cheese is melted and dish is bubbly.

Even cooking mishaps and disasters make for wonderful memories. Like the time I bit down into a peppermint Christmas cookie we'd made, only to discover some chewed bubblegum that had somehow become part of the recipe. Since we gave homemade cookies to our neighbors and friends every Christmas, I was afraid that perhaps another cookie had also received a wad of chewed bubblegum. Careful investigation never did reveal the guilty chef whose gum had fallen into the batch, and I was definitely not laughing at the time, but years later, it's one of our funniest family memories.

This is a good time to mention a saying I heard once: "If it'll be funny later, it's funny now." As a young mother, I was too serious. I never found humor in the first moments of an incident. However, when my oldest and youngest children compare notes, it seems I've managed to lighten up over the years.

Insist on working at a job you love

From the 1960s until the mid-1990s, record numbers of mothers entered the workforce to help support their families. In the 2000s, many women are waiting longer to get married and have children. At the same time, fathers are sharing more household duties and spending more time with their children.

Many parents work at full-time jobs and raise children at the same time. Some folks still believe that mothers should stay at home and bear all the work of caring for the home and children while the father supports the family financially. Others believe that to stay afloat financially, both parents must work. The bottom line is that someone must work to support the family financially. Whether this is one or both parents, the challenge to harmonize work and family is still important. Sociologists and psychologists agree that the road to gender equality is bumpy and uneven. In most households, childrearing and household duties are still thrust upon the shoulders of the mother, although many other lifestyle configurations have emerged.

Some stay-at-home dads have relocated their work to home offices so they can be the primary caregivers while Mom works on a job away from home. Other stay-at-home dads devote their time to home schooling and childcare, while their wives serve as the sole income provider. And in some cases, both parents work from home, where they arrange their time to allow for childcare and family activities.

Regardless of which style you choose, your attitude toward work is critical. You owe it to your family to choose work you enjoy. Managing your family and your career are challenging enough without enduring a job you don't enjoy. You don't have to choose between doing what you love and making a living. Choose to make a living by doing what you love. This will enable you to enjoy the time you spend with your family. Your family deserves a happy person, not a resentful grumpy parent who spends the day being miserable and distressed.

How to find the work you love

1. Get to know yourself and the interests that ignite your passion.
2. Follow your passion to build your confidence.
3. Build your confidence so you will increase your skills and expertise in the area you're passionate about.
4. Combine your passion, confidence, and expertise to attract a way to earn money doing what you love.

Here are four reasons why a job you love helps your family.

1. *You are better prepared to spend quality time with your family.* When you have a job you love, you're less likely to seek an unhealthy escape when you come home from work. Unfortunately, many people who hate their jobs spend money and time trying to escape the stress of their jobs by drinking or seeking escapist entertainment, which can take them away from their families physically, emotionally, or mentally, even during their time off.
2. *You'll have the energy and disposition to be a fair and loving parent.* Working on a job you hate saps your energy and probably gives you feelings of failure and powerlessness. When you arrive home, it's all too easy to try to exert the little authority you

do have in an unfair way over your children and spouse. The stress you experience on a job you don't like will also affect your emotional and physical health. A parent or spouse who has diminished health is not emotionally available. A parent who is increasingly unhappy at work is more likely to be irritable, argumentative, and sometimes even violent.

3. *Your children learn from you how to handle life's stresses.* Children are keen observers. They can tell your mood from your facial expression when you arrive home or pick them up at school. Even if you help them with their homework or serve dinner to them, they sense when you're miserable and see that you're tolerating a work situation you hate. Your way of handling your life (and theirs) becomes their first lesson in how to live life.

   If you are a ticking time bomb, then your children may grow up lacking feelings of safety or not trusting other people. If you are so caught up in your career that you spend very little time with your children, they may grow up with feelings of rejection and abandonment.

4. *Your children learn from you the connection between work, harmony, and prosperity.* If you don't enjoy your job, then your children may grow up thinking that work is something they shouldn't even expect to enjoy. They may also grow up believing they're going to have to choose between doing

what they love and making a living. That would be a shame, wouldn't it?

When you have a job, career, or business you love, your children can be involved and learn from your experiences. When we had a family business, my children helped with mailings, managing the office, running the copier, answering the telephone, and maintaining the building. My son still jokes about his stamp-licking days.

Manage your time well

Managing a family is much like running a business. When you add an outside job to family management, you have a situation that requires superior time management.

When I wanted to return to school to earn my Ph.D., my two oldest children were five and two. Many people thought I should wait until they grew up before I returned to graduate school. After all, I was already teaching full time. How, they asked, would I be able to manage work, graduate school, and two young children? I was fortunate to have a supportive husband, but it was still a challenge.

When I learned that one of the parents at violin lessons was finishing up her doctorate, I ran to catch up with her one day. I don't remember exactly what I asked her, but it was something about how she managed her doctoral studies and her family.

She said it was all about managing time well. Then, although she didn't know me, she said, "You can do it."

That sealed my commitment. I decided I was going

for my Ph.D., full speed ahead. I didn't know at the time how I would pay the tuition or how I would manage my teaching career and my children. All I knew was that I would do it. And I did. Thanks to a full grant that offered a small stipend and had the stipulation that I become a full-time graduate student, I resigned from my teaching job and spent the next four years juggling my studies and family activities. What an exhilarating ride!

It amazes me when folks say "I didn't have time" to justify their failure to get something completed. The truth is that we all have the same amount of time—168 hours a week, to be exact. What's fascinating is that one person can complete a sculpture, compose a song, or send off a book proposal in the same one-week time frame that others will say wasn't "enough time."

Don't get me wrong. Using your time wisely doesn't mean working nonstop or meditating all day. On the contrary—it means harmonizing your time to get things done that matter to you. Taking a nap can be a very good use of your time when you need to rejuvenate your body. Spending several hours writing a business plan is a very good use of time to ensure the success of your business. Singing a lullaby to your baby is an investment of your time that will pay off in immeasurable ways.

One good way to evaluate your use of your time is to keep track of what you do for one whole day. Then decide which of those actions advanced your business or personal life. Those that didn't advance either one can be eliminated in the future.

TAKE CHARGE OF YOUR TIME

Set short- and long-term goals and create a weekly schedule for your regular activities. If you're a woman harmonizing family and career, you need to put "fun and relaxation" on your calendar before anything else. Then make a promise to yourself to keep these appointments. Many men already know to do this. You see them jumping around the basketball court every Saturday.

Be flexible and sensible. You can reschedule and rearrange activities, but it's not a good idea to keep putting more and more things into your 168 hours without eliminating something.

Make a to-do list each night for the next day. Prioritize it. Do what's essential first. Carry leftover items from one day to the next if you have to. If something on your list remains undone for a full week, then you either don't want to do it and should drop it or you need to reevaluate its priority. Maybe it should be a goal for next month or next year.

Post a family calendar where the whole family can see what's coming up for the week or month. That way, everyone can see all the activities that must be coordinated and are more likely to be invested in them getting done. When I returned to graduate school, I had to plan very carefully in order to balance my home and academic life. Meeting academic deadlines was critical, but so was picking up my munchkins from preschool, going to violin lessons, feeding my household, and doing many other household chores.

To reach your goals, you're going to have to decide what's important to you and give up what isn't. While I was in school, I gave up the notion of having a spotless home, going to movies, and wearing designer clothes—especially when we decided to have our third child while I was in my second year of doctoral studies.

Don't allow your life to be interrupted or guided by someone else's priorities or emergencies. Stop rescuing folks who get themselves into the same fix on a regular basis—things like running out of gas, running out of money before payday, and so on. These people drain not only your time, but also your energy and brainpower. And plan ahead. You know your car requires gas to run, for example, and you know you won't have time to get it on the way to an appointment. Fill up the day before.

By the way, you aren't still answering those telemarketing calls, are you? You do have Caller ID on your phone by now, right? Turn off your cell phone when you're engaged in an important activity. That's why you have voice mail, right? Don't return calls from folks you don't want to talk to. It doesn't make you a bad person; just a smart, purpose-driven person.

When we were raising four children, there was a period when we had a child in high school, one in middle school, one in elementary school, and a baby in preschool, all at the same time. My husband and I were both working; so on school days we all had to follow a tight schedule if we were going to get to our destinations on time. In addition, we had to be sure everyone had their completed homework, signed forms to return to the teacher, lunches, violins on orchestra day, the stack of newspapers for the paper drive, and so on.

The only way we pulled all this off was through careful planning the night before. Anything that was going with us the next day went in the car the night before... except the children, of course. The next morning, everyone had to show up fully dressed for breakfast since I could whip up breakfast faster than a short-order cook. Once in the car, we started our "chauffeur service," dropping children off at their schools and, when we had only one car, dropping one spouse off at work.

Being happy and successful is not a matter of luck. It's a matter of doing what is most important to you minute by minute, day by day. If you don't manage your time, then other people will. And guess whose priorities they will put first.

Plan time away from your children. You love them, but to maintain your sanity, you need time away from them. This idea didn't sit well with my husband at first. I had to drag him away from the children so we could have a weekend alone. His thinking was that we'd have plenty time to be alone once the children were grown. My thinking was that if we waited that long, I wouldn't want to be alone with him.

Not taking time to nurture their relationship as a couple is a mistake many parents make, but taking that time is one of the most important parts of maintaining a happy life. The daily stress of working, managing your household, and dealing with life's challenges can bring on unhappy situations if you don't plan for some relief. Some couples plan a "date night" at regular intervals, weekly or every other week. They hire a babysitter and go out to dinner and a movie or even take an occasional weekend vacation. There are infinite ways to find some time away from the children. Experiment and find what works for you.

Also plan time alone. Just as it's important to take a break from your children, it's equally important to take a break from everyone and be alone. When my youngest two children went away to a church camp for four days, I was home alone. I resisted my habitual temptation to fill my time to the brim, and instead decided to sleep late, read books I wanted to read, and watch several movies I'd wanted to see. When they returned, energized and invigorated from their time away, I was rested and rejuvenated from the "me" time I'd had.

Clarify your values

What do you find most important in life? What do you value? Your values will determine how you manage your family and work.

Some of the things I value are learning, harmony, creativity, spirituality, research, music, fashion, humor, inspiring others, socializing with family and friends, and creating an inviting environment. Because our family valued learning, it was important that our children attended school, completed homework, and mastered concepts. Families who put a high importance on politics, on the other hand, may stress that their children become knowledgeable and conversant about local, national, and world news. Clarify your priorities and teach them to your children.

Get real

Before you got married and had a family, you probably had unrealistic expectations of what your life would be like. I know I did. As you watched toddlers throwing tantrums in the grocery store or saw your friends' kids watching hours of TV, you probably vowed that you were not going to be "that" kind of parent. You probably also thought you'd never yell at your children, spank them, or let your children see you get angry.

Get real. If you try to hold to unrealistic expectations, you'll need professional help to untangle the psychological bind you've put yourself in.

Your children can survive and thrive with authentic parents who exhibit real emotions and real, human flaws. Along with being real with yourself, you'll allow your children to be real. Having perfect grades and a well-kept room are not guarantees of a happy and fulfilling life. Pay more attention to grooming your and their insides than the outsides.

If you live long enough to become a grandparent, then you can enjoy the hero's role. When asked why grandparents and grandchildren get along so well, someone once said it's because they have a common enemy.

Give up the fantasy of being a perfect parent

You are going to make mistakes, upset your kids, and discover that Mary Poppins was a great movie—but she's not a template for real life. Because I grew up in the era of perfect TV parents like Ozzie and Harriet, I began my family with ridiculous expectations.

When I had my second child, I realized I needed help if I were to continue teaching. I put an ad in the local paper and got eight responses. If I didn't already believe in God, I would have become a believer the day Mrs. Morgan came into our lives. She was around seventy years old, still drove her own car, lived about a mile away, and was willing to come to our home every day as we left for work.

The first time I met her, I went to her home. As soon as she opened the door and saw my second daughter in my arms, she grabbed her and said, "Here's my baby," and immediately began baby-talking with her. Everything about our first meeting told me she was the right person to help me with my children.

Mrs. Morgan must have had a big laugh after I left that first day. I had prepared a list of rules, including the baby's schedule and all kinds of emergency information. I was in my early twenties, still a relatively new mom, and there she was; she had raised two children (who were older than I was), been babysitter to countless others, and knew more about raising children than Dr. Spock in all his wisdom. Over time, she became another grandmother to my children and another mother to me and my husband. She continued to be our babysitter through two more children and was a beloved friend of our family until her death.

Let go of the guilt

Don't trap yourself into feeling guilty about leaving your children in preschool or with a babysitter while you're at work. Or feeling guilty that you're neglecting your job when you're with your family.

If you work for a company, you've made an agreement to get certain tasks and activities completed in exchange for compensation. In the process, however, you've hopefully worked out how time off, sick leave, and vacations will be carried out. Communicate honestly with your boss about your work hours and family commitments and negotiate ways for you to meet your full obligations without stress or neglect. When you're at work, give your work your full undivided attention.

Suzy Welch (2009), former editor-in-chief of *Harvard Business Review* and work-life columnist for *O the Oprah Magazine,* was often faced with dilemmas where parenting her four children and the demands of her career intersected. If you're a working mom, you'll immediately relate to being torn between leaving the kids with a babysitter while you scurry off to give an important presentation that will further your career or hauling them to work or cross country with you. She discovered that making decisions was easier by considering the short- and long-term consequences in the next 10 minutes, 10 months, 10 years.

The technique begins with a question. Should I quit my job? Should I sell my possessions and travel the world with kids in tow? Should I accept this promotion? Should I go to the gym today? Should I hold my daughter back one school year? Then consider the impact of these in 10 minutes, 10 months, 10 years. You can think this through, write it out, or discuss it with friends. Just be thorough and honest.

Going to the gym won't have much impact on my next 10 minutes, but if I'm consistent, it'll surely have a positive impact on my health and life in 10 months, and in 10 years will enable me to live independently and enjoy a high quality of life in my retirement.

Welch explained how she came up with this technique and how it saved her parenting and her life. She also rolled out many case studies showing how others successfully are using this technique.

Regardless of the decisions you make, it's important to do what I call Be Here Now. In other words, when you're at work, give it your undivided attention. When you leave work, prepare to give your family your full attention. Some of us accomplish this by taking some time to make the transition, like spending a few minutes of quiet before launching into all the tasks that await you at home. Remember how 1960s American children's TV host Mr. Rogers always changed into his cardigan sweater and sneakers when he entered his TV house? My adult kids now tell me they understand why that transition was so necessary.

RESPECT THE SACREDNESS OF YOUR HOME

Create a loving environment and keep toxic people and things out. Toxic people always make you feel unhappy, depressed, discouraged, and tired. They enjoy dumping their negative stories, adventures, complaints, and fault-finding on you. Once they do, you may notice that they seem relieved, maybe even relaxed and cheerful, but that's only because they've given you their poison. If you tried to comfort them, maybe they sucked up some of your positivity and left you empty. Psychic vampires are not good for us. The problem is that after they've gone away, you're still feeling down and their negative energy is still reverberating through your home.

Just as you wouldn't knowingly expose your family to harmful viruses, poison ivy, or caustic fumes, don't unknowingly expose them to the negativity of toxic people and psychic vampires. While it may be true that the ones you know are suffering from mental problems, it isn't your job to cure them, and you certainly can't drag them to therapy.

You owe it to yourself and your family to keep these toxic people away because there is no way to have them in your space without being poisoned by their negativity. This is true even if some of your relatives fall into this unfortunate group. While it's tougher keeping negative relatives away, it's critical to your happiness.

Drawing clear boundaries is one way to keep these folks away. Maintaining your positive attitude and countering their negative talk with positive talk is another way. But for the hardcore bottom feeders who only get pleasure from releasing evil thoughts and behavior, you may have to tell them clearly and in easy-to-understand language that they are not welcome in your home.

I used to lament the fact that I only saw certain relatives at funerals and never socialized with them otherwise. As I grew older and wiser, I realized that there was a good reason for that. They were toxic, and I didn't want my children exposed to the ones who enjoyed dredging up painful events, gossiping about whoever was absent from the gathering, and reveled in recounting how that person had cheated, hurt, or maligned someone. Fortunately, they didn't want to be around my efforts to be cheerful, positive, and happy, so we stayed apart.

A friend of mine who was a social psychologist once said that when you feel bad after having been in someone's company, you have just been emotionally abused.

Toxic people certainly have a right to live their lives as they wish, but so do you. Make a decision to invite positive and uplifting people into your home and your life. Expose your family to people who are living wonderful, inspiring, and engaging lives. You didn't get to choose your relatives, but you can choose the company you keep. If some of your relatives aren't people you want to spend time with, wish them well, love them from a distance.

USE SOME OF YOUR MONEY TO CREATE LASTING MEMORIES RATHER THAN COLLECTING TRANSITORY THINGS

When my husband passed away, my younger two children received his Social Security benefits. The paperwork that comes with the benefits includes a list of acceptable ways to use the money. Two that stuck out for me were their education and their entertainment. I decided then that I would use the money to create memories that would stay with them throughout their lives.

First, we went on a cruise to the Mexican Rivera for the Fourth of July. It was the first time we had not celebrated this holiday by barbecuing at home with the family. I was a little concerned that stepping away from the traditional celebration would feel strange, but that went away as we watched the dolphins do their graceful dance outside our window by our table in the formal dining room. Later, exploring the many shipboard activities and touring the cities of Mazatlan and Puerto Vallarta when we docked were amazing. The most amazing was snorkeling for the first time in Cabo San Lucas. Another year, we went to Disney World and then on a cruise to the Bahamas. Another time, we spent Thanksgiving in Hawaii. We will always remember those trips and our adventures because we stepped away from the usual to embrace new experiences, sample new foods, and learn about new cultures.

TAKE LOTS OF PICTURES THROUGHOUT THE YEARS

My husband and I often disagreed about this because it does take time to stop what you're doing for pictures. But you realize later that it was worth the time. You don't have to be a great photographer, and you don't always have to go for posed pictures. Whether you put photos of your family in your office, make scrapbooks, send them to friends, share them online, or hang them on the wall, you will always be happy later that you took them. As soon as the children were born, we began taking photos of every milestone, from potty training to first and last days of school. Whether they were performing in recitals, participating in church programs or camping with the scouts, we filled photo albums with loads of photos. Friends and relatives were part of the photos as well when we were visiting and celebrating together.

When digital cameras became available, I must admit that I took even more photos, but stored most of them on flash drives and CDs, only printing select ones. Best of all, I now have photos to create my own Christmas cards. For a few decades, I have also chronicled the activities of that year in a poetic form to go along with the photo. My clumsy poetry won't win any prizes, but the annual updates delight family and friends.

Keep a camera or your smartphone nearby at all times. Don't just take pictures of special occasions. Random, candid shots often make some of the most precious and memorable photos. The smartphone with its high quality camera has made it so much easier to capture these moments as still shots and/or video, and share them right away with family and friends. Don't rely just on sharing them online however. Back up your photos on a flash drive, CD, and other places in case any one of these methods crashes.

> Color your life *flamboyant* with orange.
> It's the color of fun and energy.

SUMMARY

Juggling career and family is a challenging but worthwhile endeavor. After all, the reason most of us work is to provide for our families. But if you provide your family only with material goods and neglect to give of yourself, then you have missed the mark when it comes to creating happiness.

To accomplish the balance you seek, you must intend to make it happen and make balance a lifelong commitment. Once you've set these two goals, it's easier to get involved with your children's lives.

Additionally, you will find a great source of strength and help in creating harmony in life if you create a spiritual partnership. As a result of this partnership, you may attend church, pray, or meditate regularly, or take nature walks. No matter what you choose, the important element is recognizing there is a higher power—someone or something greater than you that is a source of comfort and awe.

Make your family your highest priority. Whether you're considering a big move, a big purchase, or starting a new business—your decisions must be based on what will be best for your family. If you want your children to have strong roots in the community, then you may decide not to take a job that involves moving every two years. On the other hand, if your priority is to give your children a variety of experiences, such as living in different cultures, then you may seek jobs in different countries that will help you reach this goal.

Give up the fantasy of being a perfect parent, but insist on having a job you enjoy. Manage your time so you can enjoy time with your children, time alone with your spouse and away from the kids, as well as time to enjoy being completely on your own.

HAPPINESS FLASHBACK

When my son was in middle school, his school bus picked him up in our neighborhood and took him to a magnet school about twelve miles away. When we were out driving around town on weekends, he was convinced that his bus passed many intersections it could not have possibly passed. He kept insisting, "My bus stops here."

If his bus had stopped at all the places he thought, he would never have gotten to school. It became such a family joke that no matter where we traveled in the world, we'd say, "Herbert's bus used to stop here."

HANDLING CHANGE AND ADVERSITY

Hardships make or break people.
—Margaret Mitchell,
Author of *Gone with the Wind*

The start of school is an exciting time for children of all ages, and for their parents and teachers, too. Teachers prepare their classrooms with posters and handouts. College campuses buzz with freshmen moving into their dorms with the help of proud parents, and returning commuter students are searching for parking. Most school-aged kids are very concerned about being dressed in the latest and coolest fashion.

But the idea of *back to school* has changed. After retiring from full-time teaching, I began teaching an online graduate course at a local university. One semester we received an email with a subject I had never seen in school email:

Guidance for Surviving an Active Shooter Situation. Attached to the email was a twenty-minute video titled *Shots Fired on Campus—When Lightning Strikes.* In the video, a campus security officer addressed faculty, staff, and students on ways to protect themselves and develop a survival mindset in the event of campus shootings. Although the narrator stressed that campus shootings were infrequent, we knew that they wouldn't be addressing this issue if the problem had not risen to a serious level. Now, in addition to coping with bullies, we teachers were also being asked to learn how to dodge bullets and even take down a shooter.

Yes, *back to school* has changed. Schools that once downplayed or covered up violence and conflict on campuses can no longer stay in denial. The highly reported, senseless shootings at schools in recent years have led to many changes, including specialized teacher training in handling hostage situations.

There is an old saying that nothing is certain in life but death and taxes. To this we must add one more certainty: *change*.

Just as you now face airport security, you have to protect your identity online and in real life, so now school safety has changed the way you and your family live. And you can look forward to more changes as long as you're alive. Your challenge is to accept change as inevitable and find strategies for handling it. Even if you decided to sit it out for a lifetime, changes will inevitably occur. If no one lives in a room, it still gets dirty, dusty, and full of cobwebs. That's change.

What major changes can you expect in a lifetime? During your lifetime, you are likely to fall in love with someone who doesn't love you back, get cheated by someone you trusted, be rejected in a job interview, or fail a test. What else? You'll lose a contest or your keys, get stranded in a strange place, fall and scrape your knee, encounter unfriendly strangers, be called vulgar names, and watch someone you love die. As you age, your body and mind will also change. And you'll see all these things happen to your children.

How can you possibly be prepared for the horrible assaults, disasters, and other varieties of adversity that you may encounter in your life?

When your challenge seems impossible to overcome or a birth defect sets your life on a course your parents never imagined, what can you do?

> *Keep your face to the sunshine and you cannot see the shadow.*
>
> —Helen Keller

Many people around the world, due to birth defects or severe illnesses or accidents, find themselves physically, mentally, and psychologically challenged as they live their lives and go after their goals. Nevertheless, some create a level of happiness and well-being for themselves. You can be inspired by their tenacity and dedication to making a positive difference in the world. Here are three amazing people who, in spite of the great difficulty they faced, managed their lives to perform activities we take for granted.

Helen Adams Keller, American author, activist, and journalist, is thought to be the first deaf and blind person to receive a bachelor's degree. Born in 1880, Keller lost her sight and hearing due to a high fever at the age of eighteen months. She learned to communicate through limited sign language with the daughter of the family cook. But it wasn't until 1887, when her mother's search for help brought them into contact with Anne Sullivan, a recent graduate of the Perkins School for the Blind of Boston, that Helen's astounding progress began. It was Sullivan's skill and tenacity that helped Helen reach her potential. Their teacher-pupil friendship spanned forty-nine years. Keller graduated from Radcliffe College and went on to help found the American Civil Liberties Union. She also received honorary doctoral degrees for work towards the betterment of others. She even learned to speak, though not as normally as she always wished. Learn more about Helen Keller at http://www.hki.org/.

Stephen Hawking, a British theoretical physicist born in 1942, was diagnosed with Amyotrophic lateral sclerosis (ALS, also known as Lou Gehrig's disease) at age twenty-one, while he was still enrolled at Cambridge University. Doctors gave him two to three years to live. To date, he has been battling the disease for over fifty years. As time passed, Hawking gradually lost the use of his arms, legs, and voice, and by 2009, he was almost completely paralyzed.

In spite of his physical challenges, Hawking captured the attention of the world with his big bang theory and black hole theory and became a celebrity thanks to his books and public appearances. Never letting his physical challenge stop him, he did research, taught, and gave interviews using his eyes to choose words in a special computer program that had been preprogrammed with words he used frequently. (The computer talks for him.) With great effort, he can also create new words that aren't in his program yet. Even as his ability to communicate deteriorates, Hawking is working with Intel on a system that will speed up his communication. He is an Honorary Fellow of the Royal Society of Arts, and in 2009 received the highest civilian award in the United States, the Presidential Medal of Freedom. You can learn more about Hawking at his official website, http://www.hawking.org.uk/.

Finally, let me introduce Nick Vujicic, an Australian motivational speaker, born in 1982 without arms or legs, but with two small feet, one of which has two toes. Although he was the first handicapped person to be allowed to attend mainstream school in his area, he was bullied so much that he fell into deep depression by age eight. After a failed suicide attempt at age ten, Nick prayed for God to give him arms and legs. It wasn't until his mother showed him an article about a man who was living with a severe disability that he realized his own disability was a unique opportunity to help others. He graduated from Griffith University and speaks to corporations, congregations, and schools. He married in February 2012 and became a father in February 2013. Learn about his life in his book (Vujicic, 2010), view his videos on YouTube, and visit his website at http://nickvujicic.com/.

I don't believe that Keller, Hawking, and Vujicic created their challenges as consequences for their behavior in a former lifetime or welcomed them in this one. What they did that was remarkable was to face their conditions and carve out meaningful lives in spite of those conditions. More important, they have used their disabilities as an example to help and inspire others with similar challenges.

Blindsided at a crossroads

By 1986, my husband and I had been married 17 years and one day were having one of many arguments. He was working full time in patient relations for a health insurance company, and I had just finished work at the summer program at my tutoring center. With a quick two-week window before the fall session would begin and my kids would return to school, I wanted a break. I suggested we get away for the weekend. As usual, he objected, saying it would be frivolous, a waste of money. I countered with my usual insistence that taking a break was healthy and we both needed it. As he blurted out what seemed like ridiculous and frustrating comebacks about how we couldn't afford it or didn't have anyone who would watch the kids, I pushed back with how we couldn't afford not to take a break. We got louder and louder until he finally inserted his usual two-punch argument-ending threats:

"Get someone else to go with you!" and "I can always move out!"

Until that day, at this point in our arguments I would break down in tears, "How can you say such a thing? What kind of husband tells his wife to find someone else? That doesn't solve anything!"

Instead, the words that tumbled out of my mouth were, "How soon can you be out?"

Without realizing it, I had hit a crossroads. I was no longer willing to participate in our seemingly senseless arguments that usually circled around taking vacations, getting away, or engaging in leisure activities. He was comfortable with working hard, encouraging the kids in their homework, and other activities, as long as he could be behind the scenes. His work ethic was strong, but his ability to relax and have fun was weak.

As a matter of fact, eight years earlier he had been the driving force behind my going after and completing my doctorate, even though it meant I had to quit my full-time teaching job to take advantage of a grant. We hunkered down financially as we adjusted to just one income. For four years as I attended classes and did my doctoral research, he was content being behind the scenes cooking, babysitting the kids, and picking me up from night classes when we had to share a car. Although we had a tight budget during these years, our marriage was smoother than ever, since I was focused on my studies and the kids, and he was working behind the scenes. When I completed my studies, I insisted that he and the kids witness my dissertation orals, but a week later he refused to attend my graduation, saying he couldn't get the time off from work.

I was hurt. Even as I write this decades later, tears well up thinking that something in him wouldn't allow him to celebrate with me. And because he refused to go to marriage counseling, I never found out why or how to resolve his difficulty with celebrating my success and with spending leisure time with his family. Throughout our marriage when he would rather have stayed at home, I had insisted he attend recitals, and go with me and the kids to Yosemite, Alaska, and other vacations. Once he was there, he usually adjusted, but I was always frustrated and exhausted from having to coerce him to participate, and from feeling like he wasn't truly there, enjoying time with me.

In spite of his years of threats to leave when he felt cornered, my husband didn't really seem to have an exit plan. I'm sure he thought I would get over our last argument, as I always had in the past. From the time I uttered those fateful words, however, there was no turning back. After two awkward weeks of his being content to sleep in a back room, I gathered his clothes and insisted that he keep his word and move out.

I didn't have a big plan either, but I felt lighter and optimistic about my future.

He found an apartment and moved into it. I wasn't ready to think about a divorce since I now had to find a way to supplement the meager profits from my tutoring program. I also didn't insist on any financial support from him yet, other than occasional things for the kids.

I closed my private tutoring program within months of our separation. I needed a steady income, and quick. After a six-month job search while I navigated four part-time jobs, I was hired in August 1987 for a full-time teaching position at Fullerton College.

During the next year, we worked out a visitation schedule where I dropped the kids at his apartment on Friday evenings and he returned them home on Sunday nights. Whereas he had always wanted to stay home while I took the kids to church, now he took the kids to church every Sunday. Interesting. I decided he was playing Daddy Good-Guy to convince the kids that I was the villain who ended it all. This of course upset me, but church was good for the kids so I kept quiet.

Because my new job was a 37-mile drive from Los Angeles, I was soon ready to shorten my commute so I began house hunting in Orange County. Although I hadn't found the house I wanted yet, I decided to put my house up for sale. The "for sale" sign was planted on the lawn on a Tuesday. That next Monday, my husband died, about a year and a half after we had separated.

I had taught classes at Fullerton College that morning and had just arrived back in Los Angeles when I got the news. A doctor at the medical facility where he worked noticed my husband didn't look good that day. He gave him a quick exam, issued him a prescription, and told him to go home. He died from a heart attack in the driver's seat, before he could start his car.

By now, my oldest daughter was living on her own and my second daughter was living with her father. My youngest two were living with me.

The afternoon he died, school was already out, so I went to his apartment to wait for my second daughter to get home from school. After breaking the news her father had died, I gathered up her clothes and brought her back to live with me.

The two weeks after his death were some of the toughest of my life. I had to take my house off the market while I planned the funeral, moved my second daughter (who I discovered was pregnant) back home with me, and discovered in the midst of all this that my husband had let his two life insurance policies lapse.

After these emotional two weeks passed, I put my house back on the market and focused on supporting my second daughter in finishing high school that year. She and her boyfriend made plans for my first grandchild.

In the spring of 1989, my house in Los Angeles sold, and I found a lovely home in Orange County, California, only ten miles from my job. Two weeks before I started my second year of teaching at Fullerton College, we moved in.

Even good change can be stressful

When we moved from Los Angeles County to Orange County, I was very excited. I looked forward to living in a bigger house in a safer neighborhood surrounded by my favorite stores and conveniences. I could finally send my kids to neighborhood schools, go to clean, well-kept grocery stores, and be near the post office, a wonderful movie theater, a park, and other favorite places. Best of all—now I lived much closer to work.

I was exhilarated but still under a lot of stress. Six months after our move, I experienced a panic attack. I was driving home from church one evening when I suddenly started to feel dizzy. It got hot in the car. I began to feel like I was shrinking. Fearing that I was going to faint and cause a major car accident, I pulled over and took the next exit off the freeway.

I had only been in Orange County a few months, so I didn't know the surface-street route home. I only knew the freeway route, and this happened in the days before GPS was common. Still panicking, I pulled into the nearest gas station and asked the attendant to tell me how to get to Anaheim Hills by surface streets. But he didn't understand my question and told me how to get back to the same freeway I had just exited. All I could do was pull out of the station and park in the dark at the nearest curb. By now, I felt so foolish and helpless that I began to sob. Even though I could have called a friend who was at my house waiting for me, my customary reluctance to ask for help kept me from using my cell phone.

Even more frustrating was that I knew I was only a few freeway exits from home. But I was terrified to get back on the freeway. After a few minutes of calming my nerves, I convinced myself to get back on the freeway by reassuring myself that as soon as I recognized an exit, I would take it and finish my trip home by the surface streets. I cautiously returned to the freeway and, staying in the right-hand lane, looked anxiously at every upcoming exit. Just two exits away was one I recognized. I left the freeway and drove home. As I drove, I tried to understand what had happened to me.

Anyone who has had a panic attack probably felt confused about what was happening. What had brought the attack on? What could I do about it? When I tried to explain my experience to my doctor, I was not very successful. She prescribed pills to treat vertigo, but they were destined to make me dizzier. So I gave up on finding a medical solution and decided to use the spiritual principles I had been learning all my life. I prayed, I meditated... and I stayed off freeways for more than a year. I also researched online to discover the nature of my anxiety and find ways to handle it.

The fear of losing control is terrifying, especially when you're driving. While driving itself didn't cause my anxiety, now the anxiety was tied to driving because I had been driving when the panic attack hit.

When you live in Southern California, having driving anxiety is a major inconvenience. I still had to drive to work and to events. While I was combating my driving anxiety, I took elaborate steps to avoid the freeway. I even stayed in hotels to avoid driving at night. Eventually, I worked myself out of my driving anxiety, but then years later it returned. I decided my panic attacks came from getting overloaded and overwhelmed.

This first episode took place a few months after our move, when we not only had to relocate ourselves but also start new schools and learn to find new stores, doctors, and every other service related to daily living. As the clear decision-maker, planning and executing everything fell on my shoulders.

Typical of my go-get-'em attitude and lifestyle, I thought I had dealt with the feelings of grief and anger following my separation from my husband and his subsequent death the previous year. I simply soldiered on with what I needed to believe was superhuman strength, while my all-too-human body continued to experience all the physical stress natural for someone experiencing complicated grief and loss.

None of it felt oppressive to me at the time because I was too busy coping with all the change and the work required to pull it off to allow myself to feel oppressed by it. I had switched into survival mode, and I just piled on too much. I became overwhelmed.

The second episode occurred in 2005, the day before I was to travel to Europe for the first time. I was going to join my daughter for vacation and had scheduled my trip to begin within a few days of my last day of school. I finished grading finals, submitted grades, and did my final packing. I was running last-minute errands and headed to the last one, an appointment at the beauty shop, when the lightheadedness and fear of losing control of the car swept over me again. I promptly called my hairstylist to cancel my appointment and went to the doctor instead. After hours of extensive testing, the doctor could find no physical reason for the attack. Since I had no apparent physical problems, she gave me clearance to proceed with my vacation plans. (An upside is that I hadn't made plans to drive during my vacation. Being a passenger didn't bother me.)

A therapist would readily find it noteworthy that I was on the way to the beauty shop when this second panic attack occurred. At the time, I missed the connection, but now I wonder if it could be that growing up with all those emotional associations from my mother raising us in a beauty shop bubbled up without my realizing it. After all, I had been raised to believe I could accomplish whatever I put my mind to, but I was still learning the important skills of managing life balance and remembering to take good care of myself, even in times of stress. My mother had shown me by example that I could be a responsible parent and enjoy a fulfilling career, but I hadn't understood the complexities of life from the perspective of a busy working mother until my life had become truly challenging, both physically and emotionally. And somehow the message from my mother, busy at her beauty shop helping women look good while they talked about and struggled with the "sad" and stressful parts of life, had always seemed to focus on moving past or ignoring troubling feelings and experiences.

Instead of dwelling on anger, I was raised to smile,

push upset aside, and take care of the tasks in front of me. I'm very grateful for this lesson, as there is much life to be lived and satisfying work to be done. But coming to terms with adversities, with my anger and every other feeling I might have about them, allowing myself to express my feelings appropriately, and being gentle and forgiving of myself were essential to keeping me healthy and making life satisfying.

When I returned from my vacation, I vowed to find a way to deal with these attacks before a third one hit me. Through my research, I learned about a program called Emotional Freedom Technique (EFT). Gary Craig, the founder of EFT, readily admits he isn't a licensed therapist or psychologist. In fact, he is a Stanford engineering graduate and an ordained minister with the Universal Church of God in Southern California. While I have a strong belief in God and His power, I was drawn to this method because it is not tied to any religious beliefs. It is, in fact, based on a combination of the theories of mind-body medicine and acupuncture. In EFT, however, there are no needles or medicines involved, and it is reported to work with an infinite list of physical and other conditions.

The technique involves tapping specific meridian points on your forehead, face, chest, arms, or hands while repeating a two-part affirmation. The first part identifies the problem; the second professes self-acceptance. EFT works by acknowledging and releasing negative emotions surrounding the problem and relying upon the body's natural energy fields to heal itself. Perhaps the efficacy of these and other clinical treatments for anxiety and panic arises from simply learning to accept and honor how we feel, in order to move to a place of acceptance and peace.

You may be as skeptical as I was that something so simple, quick, and easy to do could work or have lasting effects. Some folks have to repeat the procedure more than once. For others, it works after just one session. EFT worked at ridding me of driving anxiety and enabled me to enjoy the freedom of getting around independently. You can learn more about it or download the manual for free at http://www.emofree.com.

HANDLING ANGER

> *I think it pisses God off if you walk by the color purple in a field somewhere and don't notice it.*
>
> —Alice Walker, *The Color Purple*

At some point in our lives, personal or world events cause us stress that may lead to anger. It is well documented that increased anger raises our blood pressure. In spite of this, people who respond to stressful situations with short-term anger or indignation have a sense of control and optimism that is lacking in those who respond with fear or denial.

Here are some ways to handle short-term anger that have worked for me:

1. *Agree with yourself that you can be angry for a limited time.* When I was teaching full-time, my office mate and I shared close quarters, so we agreed early on that only one of us could be pissed at a time. Whoever stomped into the office upset first was the one who got to vent. The other had to hold off until the next day (if we even remembered what we were angry about for a whole day). It worked for our entire careers together.
2. *Write a letter about the offense to the offending party.* I like to send a letter to the editor, the college president, or whoever needs to hear my take on the subject. Be prepared for a negative reaction, or having your objection disregarded. Or write a letter where you let it all hang out, but don't actually send it. I wrote a letter to my deceased mother once and then burned it. Some "experts" say write the letter, let it all out, but don't actually send it.
3. *Express your anger to the offending party as calmly as possible.* When I returned from maternity leave to my university teaching position, I learned from my substitute that one of my colleagues had been snooping around my classroom and harassing my substitute to find out what grades and assignments the students we shared received. The snooping teacher was convinced that if some of our shared students were passing my class and failing hers, then I must be too lax or incompetent or both.

This colleague's behavior was particularly upsetting, since I'm known for being accessible and very open to both colleagues and students. Besides, I had been on the faculty for two years before this event. If it came up while I was on leave, she could have called me. Why hadn't she approached me directly to discuss our classes? Grrr!

I could not relax until I had a conversation with this other teacher. It started off very calmly, but I'm afraid it escalated to a higher volume than I had planned because her excuses felt more pathetic than her behavior. When it was over, I felt good because it was out in the open and I didn't need to waste any more brain cells nursing the hurt or regretting that I hadn't dealt with it.

4. *Pick your battles. When I notice someone trying to rush to beat me to the grocery line or cut me off in traffic, I let them go first. (Okay, okay—most of the time.) I discovered long ago that decathlons aren't held in grocery stores or on the freeway.*

For all our efforts at maintaining happiness, anger will still happen. It's part of the human response and, like fear, has its place in our repertoire of feelings. Rather than be caught off guard or react in destructive or nonproductive ways, discover what responses to anger work best for you. Making exercise, relaxation techniques, and calming activities part of your routine goes a long way toward helping you handle anger in a healthy way.

You definitely don't want to suppress your anger or leave it unexpressed. Either of these can cause long-lasting physical and psychological damage, depression, anxiety, and panic attacks. People who never allow themselves to feel or express anger are ticking bombs. They're bound to blow up over something unrelated to the original anger-producing event.

If you realize that you get angry frequently, or if you feel that the world is against you, then it's time to seek professional help with anger management. You'll do yourself good, and your loved ones and friends will thank you.

FACE IT—SOME DAYS ARE GOING TO SUCK

We were on a very tight budget while I was finishing my doctorate, so it was a big financial sacrifice when I quit my job to become a full-time graduate student. Fortunately, we were able to pay our mortgage and keep our children healthy and fed, but many other things had to wait in line. I drove a used Ford station wagon which I was never sure would start. One morning, when I was scheduled to give surveys to teachers at an inner-city junior high school, it started pouring down rain. I pulled on my leather boots, darted between raindrops and jumped in the car. It started! Great!

When I arrived at the school, I stuffed the stack of surveys under my raincoat to keep them dry, grabbed my purse and the equipment I needed for the testing, and rushed toward the building. Just before I reached the door, I stepped into a puddle of water. When I pulled my dripping foot out of the puddle, I discovered the heel of my right boot had broken off! In order not to be late for my appointment, I limped down the hall and made it to the meeting on time. With damp clothes, a broken shoe, and dampened spirit, I proceeded as professionally as possible.

Boy! That morning sucked big time.

I share this story because sometimes as I promote positive thinking, encourage inner joy, and share tips for happiness, people get the wrong impression about me. Sometimes people wrongly believe I have found a way to master the art of creating perfect days, perhaps just through positive thinking. Not!

> Yes, some days are going to suck.
> One day your head will be the perfect
> landing place for bird droppings.
> You will lose your keys.
> Your child will lie to you.
> Someone will lie about you.

Being happy and claiming your inner joy is not about preventing bad things from happening. We have absolutely no control over the weather or what others do. We only have some control over how we react to the events in our lives.

How, then, do we get past these "sucky" days?

- *Be grateful for what went right.* My old car got me to and from my research appointment.

- *Choose how you react.* I was eventually able to laugh at my rainy day adventure.
- *Cry if you want.* Tears are nature's cleansing treatment.
- *Make note of what you learned.* Like, don't wear leather boots in the drenching rain.

Decades have passed since that rainy day event. Wouldn't it be a shame if I had let a single event steal my joy and color my life sad?

Adversity touches us all

When adversity strikes, it usually catches us off guard. Even though we know death is inevitable, for example, we are seldom prepared when it strikes our loved ones. Losing a loved one through death or divorce is an ending.

But it is also a beginning.

When my mother died at age ninety-two, I was grief-stricken to see her earthly life end. But that day was also the beginning of my turn to be the oldest living member of our nuclear family.

When the adversity is the loss of a job, savings, or a home, the hurt is equally painful. Again, it is an end and a beginning at the same time. Many victims of widely publicized disasters like Typhoon Haiyan (known in the Philippines as Typhoon Yolanda) and Superstorm Sandy on the East Coast feel helpless and abandoned. They decide that life is unfair. The truth is, however, that life is neutral. No one is immune from adversity. It's the cost of living life. As Jesus pointed out, we can expect *"rain on the just and the unjust."* (Matthew 5:45 World English Bible).

Responding to threats

Sometimes our intuition tries to warn us of impending danger. If we pay attention to what some people call hunches, we can sometimes avert or avoid a bad situation. Here's an example of an incident that happened to me. Several friends I had met in Italy decided to meet at a hotel in El Segundo, California for a reunion. As we were returning in my car from dinner one night, I was searching for street parking. The hotel had paid parking at the rate of $20 per night, which we thought was an exorbitant fee. I couldn't find a space on the same block as the hotel, so I drove to the next block. As I was maneuvering my car to parallel park, four young men appeared from around the corner, walking down the sidewalk toward us. At the same time, we saw a car with its interior lights on moving slowly down the street. The driver glanced over at the four young men walking toward us. Just as I was about to straighten my car in the parking space, a red flag went off in my head. We were in danger!

"Don't open the door," I said to the ladies. I immediately got the car out of that space and zoomed down the street. "We're going to pay to park tonight!"

To this day, I have no doubt we were about to be robbed… or worse.

When adversity strikes, you can do several things:

- Keep your cool.
- Evaluate the situation.
- Decide on a positive and healthy action to take.
- Avoid wallowing in self-pity or playing the victim.
- Focus on what you have, not what you've lost.
- Afterward, write down as many details of the incident as possible. Stories of how you overcame adversity are appealing, especially on job and scholarship applications. They show your strengths.

Don't like where you are? Make a getaway plan.

Have you ever been in a job or relationship you wanted to escape? Chances are, you groused about it for a while before doing anything about it. Or perhaps you are the rare bird who leaped out of it instantly and found yourself in an emotional or financial freefall.

When you discover you're unhappy and unfulfilled in a job, relationship, or other situation, it might be a good idea to make a getaway plan before you make a move.

My oldest daughter once had the miserable experience of being on a job where she wasn't appreciated. Even worse, she was not given the training she was promised, so she found herself muddling along, trying to learn the job on the job. Her supervisors and coworkers were not much help. She discovered their reluctance to help, and their negative remarks masked their own incompetence.

The atmosphere was unfriendly and discouraging, but she had just moved to the town to take the job, and she had bills to pay and wanted to complete the probationary period before changing jobs.

No matter what your job is, there are probably aspects of it you don't like. Many people work in an atmosphere so toxic that they dread going to work. Some even become physically sick from the anticipation and actuality of emotional abuse. What can you do when you're stuck in a negative work environment? Most people would quickly retort, "Quit! Get another job."

Depending on your risk tolerance level, you may not be one who's able to put up with an intolerable situation for even one day. But my daughter had a low tolerance for risk, and quitting immediately didn't seem like an option to her. Yet she had to do something. Along with two other new coworkers who were equally unhappy and shared her desire to escape, she created a getaway plan. Here are four steps she took.

First, she outlawed any negative talk in her cubicle. Before she laid down the law, she and her two coworkers spent a disproportionate part of their time together complaining about all the things they hated about the job. Now they could only step into her cubicle if they had something positive to share.

Second, she created a lunchtime support group. During these times, the three of them shared

- Tips on revising their résumés
- Job announcements they had discovered for each other
- Articles about dealing with office politics
- Tips on interviewing
- Inspirational and motivational articles

  And they created a notebook of the information they shared. They kept their revised résumés in one section of the notebook, ready to be submitted when they spotted a desirable opening somewhere else.

Third, she suggested they take up positive hobbies that could relieve their stress. My daughter taught herself to crochet. By Christmas that year, she had made scarves for every family member. Her two friends took up knitting. They, too, had stacks of handmade gifts to give to friends and family that year.

Fourth, she enrolled in every free training the company offered. This enabled her to learn new skills at company expense while also getting time away from her negative office environment.

By the time my daughter and her coworkers had successfully completed their probationary period, they no longer hated to come to work. It wasn't because the office environment had suddenly become welcoming and positive, but now they looked forward to seeing each other and working on their getaway plans. The time they spent together had tremendous benefits, too. They

- Discovered specific things they didn't like on the current job
- Detailed what they wanted on their new jobs
- Built new skills they could use on the next job
- Became more selective about which job openings to pursue
- Refined their résumés
- Polished their interviewing skills

By taking these four steps, they learned to look forward to going to work. Now they could continue to pay their bills and enjoy medical benefits while patiently crafting their getaway plans. And, sure enough, one by one, my daughter and her coworkers found the new jobs they now enjoy. During that year of making their getaway plans, they succeeded at more than just finding new jobs. They discovered new inner strengths, resilience, and strategies that will serve them well in their personal and professional lives for many years.

What about when you hit rock bottom?

> *In our life there is a single color, as on an artist's palette, which provides the meaning of life and art. It is the color of love.*
>
> —Marc Chagall

As an African-American woman, I notice that many ethnic minorities don't seem to get as upset during economic downturns as many in the white majority seem to.

I think this is because we've known poverty and don't fear it as much as people who have never been really poor. Because we have come from a history of enslavement and many rights denied, we go into survival mode when our money dwindles. Nowadays, many of us have never faced abject poverty. We live very comfortable lives, but we still know how to be poor without having it undo us. We don't define our lives by our money, but by our ability to find meaning and joy with the money we have.

The Great Recession of December 2007 to June 2009 was particularly devastating since it affected many who were most vulnerable to a downturn. Baby boomers nearing retirement and those who lost their jobs were unable to make up for the loss. Even those who continued to work reacted to the economic changes by cutting back on spending, postponing purchases, and seeking frugal alternatives, things that low income earners have done all along.

My mother always lived as if she was in a recession because she remembered the Great Depression of 1920–1939. No matter how much money she had, she was never foolhardy. No matter how little money she had, my mother always had savings. She developed her talents to cook, sew, and grow, and to can vegetables and fruit each year. My sisters and I used to laugh at the way she treated aluminum foil like gold, washing it and reusing it so it would last longer.

Families, neighbors, and church members from my

childhood also shared with one another. For example, when one neighbor's husband abandoned her, leaving behind five children to feed, neighbors brought food and clothing along with the sympathy and comfort.

When a child was left without a parent, the child was often taken in by another family and blended into the family as another sibling. When I traced our family history to create a family tree, I discovered that one of my cousins was one such child who, though not a blood relative, had been raised as one.

When I was growing up, my mother's home-based beauty shop was in the front room of our house, and we lived in the remaining rooms. There were two bedrooms, a bathroom, and a kitchen. It was common in those days for a beautician to be the sounding board for her customers' ideas and the counselor for their problems. In addition, my mother was sometimes even the banker for women who wanted to save money and keep it out of the hands of their abusive and violent husbands.

My mother and other old-timers also had strong Christian faith and hope for better times that stemmed from their slave ancestry. Since church was the one place slaves were allowed to gather, worship service was a major part of slave life and a source of hope. It is said that during slavery, slave masters encouraged field slaves to sing so they knew where they were. So the slaves sang, but they used their singing to make the work go easier and as encouragement. Slave songs soon evolved into a sophisticated code for survival and communication that enabled many to escape to freedom. In spiritual and gospel songs, for example, the word "chariot" refers to a train, and the "gospel train" is the Underground Railroad. "Wade in the Water" was Harriet Tubman's warning to runaway slaves to move into the water, where the owners' dogs couldn't follow their scent. There is an old Negro spiritual, "I'm so Glad Trouble Don't Last Always," that points to the impermanence of adversity. It reminds us that just as the good times don't last forever, neither do the bad times.

Nerburn (1999) presented a series of poignant essays of wisdom, advice, and insights about the many critical periods in life. Although directed at boys, his rich wisdom applies to all of us. I was struck by his advice that we not let hard times and poverty make us bitter and angry. It's work, no matter how menial, that helps us defeat the desperation that can come with hard times. Work gives us a platform on which we can begin to rebuild our lives.

Most important, Nerburn stressed that we must hold on to a belief in our own promise. It's our belief in our own promise that enabled many blacks and other ethnic minorities and immigrants to survive times of harsh, unfair, and cruel treatment.

The Plight of Lottery Winners

> *Fortune does not change men, it unmasks them.*
>
> —Suzanne Necker

Almost everyone thinks life would be happier if there were lots more money in the bank. Every time there is a huge jackpot, like the $590.5 million Powerball jackpot in Florida in May 2013, there is always a rush to buy tickets. Even though the chances of winning are extremely low, the thought of winning makes the $2 investment well worthwhile to the players. The winner of this largest solo win in Florida's history was an eighty-four-year-old woman who said she planned to split her winnings with her son.

"If I won the lottery," said one of my coworkers at Fullerton College, "I would buy new computers for the reading lab."

"Not me," responded another teacher. "I'd quit the next day and start partying."

Most of us have imagined how winning the lottery might take away our troubles and make our lives gloriously happy. When a Chicago couple won $30 million in the state lottery in November 2011, they decided not to tell anyone, not even their kids. They continue to work, live modestly, and teach their kids a strong work ethic.

They are the exception.

Most winners are bursting to tell the world of their good fortune, and sometimes that becomes part of their undoing. Take Evelyn Adams, who won the New Jersey lottery not just once in 1985, but again in 1986, for a grand total of $5.4 million. Thanks to her gambling habit and her inability to say no to all the folks with their hands out, all of Evelyn's money was soon gone, and she now lives in a trailer. Then there is William "Bud" Post. Even though Bud won $16.2 million in the Pennsylvania lottery in 1988, he had spent it all within a year on lawsuits and failed business ventures. He now lives on his Social Security income.

People who aren't used to having money, or those who've never learned to manage money, are in the greatest danger of losing it quickly or being the victim of scam artists. They don't know the importance of planning and investigating before investing. They also don't realize the cost of maintaining a big house, a boat, or the grand lifestyle they crave. Worst of all, if they have unhealthy relationships with family and friends, surprise winnings will magnify these feelings, emotions, and interactions.

Losing fortunes doesn't just happen to lottery winners, of course. Celebrities who earn millions on one movie deal may spend lavishly, but not earn anywhere near that amount for the next few movies. The overnight millionaires in the early dot-com days often spent their new wealth as if it would never end. When it did end, many of them lost more than just their homes and cars.

Finally, there are those who come into wealth as the result of a large insurance payout or inheritance. If these recipients don't already have a healthy relationship with managing money, they are likely to squander their newly acquired abundance.

Any unexpected money that is larger than you are accustomed to brings with it emotional reactions and the urge to spend impulsively. To avoid going into a tailspin when you receive a large sum of sudden money, Bradley (2000) suggested the following:

- Stay calm and don't make decisions based on your emotions.
- Seek experienced, professional advice.
- Avoid pressure from others.
- Create and execute the best financial plan for you.

Each of us has a happiness set point that we return to after both a huge letdown and an exhilarating experience. Just as lottery winners don't sustain their initial exuberance, studies have shown that within a year, even after tragic accidents, many paraplegics return, if not to their former level of happiness, at least to a satisfactory level of well-being. Continuously expecting our happiness to be permanently dependent on outside events sets us up for disappointment.

> *The best color in the world is the one that looks good on you.*
>
> —Coco Chanel

What can we learn from adversity?

Although we don't seek adversity, many people believe we can learn from our mistakes, problems, and challenges. In *The Happiness Hypothesis*, Jonathan Haidt (2006) acknowledged that some adversities devastate people permanently and then wrote that adversity can be good, within limits. Researchers have turned from studying only the damaging effects of stress to looking at some of its benefits. Haidt identified three benefits of stress:

1. *Our hidden abilities emerge and our self-concepts increase as a result.* We often underestimate what we can endure. We don't know how to access our hidden resources. While it is true that some people succumb to depression and some even commit suicide when they lose family, wealth, and valued possessions, we can be encouraged by those who survive and thrive as a result.

Gill (2007) recounted how, when faced with the loss of his six-figure salary, his high-level job, the diagnosis of a brain tumor, and a series of other heartbreaking blows, he hit rock bottom. But he kept up what had once been a routine, drinking his favorite latte at a Manhattan Starbucks. He had no idea his life was about to change again. He was too deep in self-pity to notice the sign advertising a "hiring open house." But the Starbucks manager perhaps assumed he was there for a job, as hiring was in progress. He certainly must have looked downtrodden since his life was at a low. Her assumption caught him off guard, but when he realized that he did in fact need a job, he applied. She offered him a job. Thus he began a life turnaround from being a member of the "old boys' club" who felt a strong sense of entitlement and had never had to search for a job before to being a worker who initially found it challenging to learn to handle the bagels, operate the cash register, and make eye contact and genuine conversation.

Michael's experience at Starbucks gave him a newfound compassion and humility along with a way to seek and accept forgiveness and love from his children. One day when he was climbing up the subway stairs, he recognized a very wealthy but notoriously cheap man. At one time, Michael would have reached out in an effort to connect with this man, but now he brushed past him without a hint of acknowledgement. It was then that Michael realized that he was no longer driven by the insecurity and arrogance of his past.

2. *Our relationships with others change.* My sister, Mildred, was diagnosed with breast cancer at the Mayo Clinic in Phoenix, Arizona. In her search for a more affordable place for chemotherapy or radiation, she discovered the Cancer Treatment Centers of America. The Center required patients to be accompanied by a caregiver. Although she could have chosen her husband or youngest adult daughter to go with her, I was surprised when she asked me. Although our relationship had not been as close as I wish it had been through the years, I agreed to go. We went to the Center in Tulsa, Oklahoma.

The Cancer Treatment Centers are amazing facilities. There are locations in Pennsylvania, Illinois, Oklahoma, Georgia, and Arizona. The organization was started in the early 1980s by Richard J. Stephenson following the tragic death of his mother, Mary Brown Stephenson, from cancer. He was so disappointed with his failure to find the loving care he wanted for his mother that he vowed to start a cancer treatment center that would treat the whole person in a compassionate and nurturing environment. Their motto is, "We treat you like we would our own mother." From the moment you enter the lobby, it's apparent that this motto is a living, breathing mission with every staff member you meet.

Our experience together at the Center gave my sister and me a new view of our relationship. I felt myself become more accepting of our differences, and she saw that our love as sisters transcended those differences. As we recognized that being a caregiver is more than giving of your time, she thanked me over and over, saying, "I have the greatest sister in the world." Even though I suspected that her feelings of gratitude would subside once we left the Center and returned to our separate homes, I was glad that we had enjoyed this rare and brief period of mutual acceptance.

3. *Our values, priorities, and perception change.* The year before I retired from my teaching career, I was considering teaching for a little longer. I had been teaching at Fullerton College close to twenty years; and while that may seem like a substantial amount of time, it wouldn't give me full retirement. I would have to teach a total of thirty years or more to reach a retirement income nearly equivalent to my salary.

During the summer of 2006, I decided to have some home remodeling done while I had ample equity in the home and so the changes would be in place when I retired.

It was one of the hottest summers on record for Southern California. Then—wouldn't you know it?—my home air conditioner broke down. The repair service was backed up with orders and wouldn't get to me for more than a week. So for more than a week, I endured the heat all day while work crews were in and out of my house doing the remodeling. It was worse at night, when it seemed to get hotter. I got so hot it was impossible for me to get cool. I didn't learn until later that I had suffered heat stroke.

Just when I felt better and the remodeling was complete, I returned to the fall semester, still not sure whether it would be my last year. My doctor had been urging me to get a colonoscopy ever since I had turned fifty, but I had neglected to do so until that fall. I made an appointment, did all the body-cleansing prep, and went to have the colonoscopy procedure, accompanied by my youngest daughter.

After I regained consciousness, the doctor told me she had removed three polyps from my colon, one of which was cancerous. Although the polyps had been removed, my doctor suggested that I should consider colon surgery to ensure that the cancer had not penetrated my colon wall.

It was then, after my heat stroke and the possibility of colon surgery, that it became clear to me: I was going to retire right now and get busy doing things I had put off for retirement. I decided to forgo surgery and improve my eating habits and lifestyle instead.

Even though I had traveled and already done many things in my life, many things remained on my list.

Postponing these things in an effort to ensure that I had a few more dollars in my retirement fund seemed ludicrous. I chose to live, love, and play more.

So I retired in May 2007 and immediately traveled to two places I had long wanted to see: China and Italy. I took several domestic trips as well. After gallivanting around the globe a bit, starting new websites and blogs, I also began writing this book.

Is there any way to prepare for stress and adversity?

While it's clear that we can't avoid adversity, we can take some steps that will lessen our discomfort and sometimes even stave off disaster… or at least help us bounce back. Most of my college students in wheelchairs were very adept at getting around campus and to and from home using their own power. Here are some things you can do to prepare for adversity:

1. *Have a support team of family, friends, and neighbors, plus church and other sources.* It's difficult to be objective and see solutions when you're caught up in your own emotionally charged situation. Having others around to see things more clearly brings tremendous relief, sometimes just because they listen, bring us a cup of tea, or sit quietly nearby.
2. *Anticipate what might happen, when reasonable and possible, without catastrophizing.* If you drive a car,

it's wise to have a roadside assistance service in case your car breaks down. In our neighborhood, we experience occasional power outages during which the electricity goes out for an hour or more. In preparation for these times, we place flashlights, candles, and matches where we can find them in the dark. If I'm working on the computer, I save my data frequently so I don't lose a lot of my work in the event of one of these outages.

3. *Plan ahead.* Insurance was created for the inevitable and unexpected. Although some people see it as burdensome because of the cost, it can be a relief when a triggering event occurs. Here's an example. When my mother died at age ninety-two, it was an emotional blow for the whole family. It's not that we don't realize that our loved ones (and we) will eventually die; it's just that we're never quite ready. Add to this the stress of preparing and paying for a funeral, and you have a tense situation. But my mother had planned and paid for her own funeral long before her death. The only decision I had to make was the type of flowers. I also had to change the soloists she had hoped would sing because both passed away before she did. I was grateful and relieved that she had taken care of so many details.
4. *Have a Plan B.* Even great actresses have understudies. Here are some examples of Plan B's. Unless you live in an area that has only one road in and out, learn alternate routes home or to work. Become

familiar with the locations of your nearest police departments. Plan for disaster. Emergency agencies warn families to have bottled water, blankets, and other supplies boxed for quick access in case of evacuation during a fire, storm, hurricane, and other natural disasters.

5. *Keep yourself in as good shape as possible.* You may have to move fast, or at least move under your own steam one day. You don't have to be a marathoner, bodybuilder, or athlete, though. I'm referring to basic health and common sense behavior. The more you can take care of your health, the better it will be for you later. Eating a healthy diet, drinking lots of water, and getting adequate sleep are the foundation of keeping yourself well. (I'm working on this one.)

Is adversity good for us?

It seems irresponsible and cruel to suggest that adversity is good for us. There is nothing ennobling about poverty and pain that would cause me to recommend them.

While it's true that many people who overcome adversity seem to live better lives, it's equally true that trauma, disaster, and adversity overtake and even destroy the lives of others. During a time of economic downturn, a common source of frustration and devastation for many families is an impending foreclosure, a job loss, or the loss of retirement savings. Domestic violence, suicide, and murder-suicides increase.

During adversity and crisis, we learn things about ourselves that can help us do better in the future. If we don't learn the lesson from adversity, we will repeat it, perhaps many times. You can probably think of an adverse situation in which you have found yourself more than once. Perhaps you even asked yourself, "How did I get here again?" The way you cope with a crisis (either a first-time or repeated event) may determine whether it comes back to revisit you. There's much evidence that evading the pain by covering it with alcohol, drugs, or denial is both temporary and detrimental.

When you are able to take a hard look at the crisis, evaluate and take action that can get you out of it. Here are some strategies that have worked for others:

1. Seek comfort and help from your friends and family.
2. Cry for as long and loud as you want. When my husband died, I cried for hours several nights in a row. Tears wash away lots of hurt.
3. Join or seek help from organizations created to help with your specific crisis, such as Mothers Against Drunk Drivers (MADD) or World Trade Center Survivors' Network (WTCSN).
4. Get relief and a fresh perspective after a massage or facial.
5. *Draw comfort and relaxation from being near or on a river, lake, or ocean.*

The passage of time brings with it distance and

healing. In the meantime, find out what works to relieve stress and help you overcome adversity, and you'll be more ready for difficult life changes as they arise.

> *Why should one complain if he is detained and imprisoned here? From ancient times, heroes often were the first ones to face adversity.*
>
> —Anonymous Chinese prisoner at Angel Island

Summary

Learning to deal with change and adversity is essential to learning to be happy. Not one of us will escape the stressful situations that cause upsets, and maybe even setbacks, in life. Knowing this, it's important to be prepared for change and adversity as a part of everyday life.

Even the wonderful things we eagerly pursue and anticipate can bring on debilitating stress. Ask any bride planning a large wedding while trying to balance her preferences with those of her husband and the two families involved—there's an example of happiness-induced stress!

It's easier to deal with anxiety when the people in your life are supportive. It's also beneficial to have plans to deal with these unwanted upsets in life. For example, if you can't get out of a bad situation immediately, you can create a getaway plan. This may lessen some stress, and the strategies you put in place can result in a successful resolution of the problem.

You're more resilient than you think. It's during the hard and down times that your strengths and abilities will emerge, perhaps to your surprise. You may find that as a result of overcoming these adversities, your relationships and priorities will change.

The best way to prepare for adversity is to recognize that it happens to us all. Accept this without becoming paranoid, make plans for the inevitable changes that come with adversity, and know that your strength to overcome will emerge when needed.

HAPPINESS FLASHBACK

One day when Tamra, my oldest, was a toddler, she declared, "When I grow up, I'm going to marry Daddy."

"You won't be able to," I informed her.

"Why not?" she asked.

"Because he's already married," I said.

"He is? Who is he married to?" she asked.

"Me," I said.

She dropped her head sadly.

HONORING YOUR INNER LEADER

No man is free who is not a master of himself.
—Epictetus

When I was growing up in St. Louis, my mother took Tuesdays off from her beauty shop business to run errands, which often meant shopping downtown. If it was a time when my sisters and I were on spring or summer break from school, she left us with strict instructions to stay indoors, not invite any company to visit, and finish our chores. We didn't own a car back then, so she had to catch the bus, which meant we could count on her trip taking most of the day.

As the oldest, I was instructed to take the lead in enforcing her rules during her absence by keeping my two younger sisters in line.

It seldom turned out well.

My second sister, Sonja, and I chose to follow Mom's instructions, but my youngest sister, Mildred, took Mom's absence as an opportunity to disappear into the neighborhood to visit her friends and have loads of unsupervised fun. No amount of pleading and warning on my part could deter her. Within minutes after our mother left, Mildred slipped out the front door and dashed out of sight.

Sonja and I always waited nervously for Mildred to return, hoping she'd get back before Mom did, thereby avoiding punishment accompanied by yelling. But she never did. She always lost track of time, and without any regard for the consequences, she was not there when Mom came home.

Mom always immediately noticed that Mildred wasn't there. "Where is Mildred?" she always asked.

"I don't know," I always stammered, fearing what was coming next. Sonja slowly backed away so the spotlight of our mother's gaze could fully focus on me.

"I left you in charge!" she always reminded me. "You're the oldest. I expected you to make sure she followed the rules."

I always resented this unwelcome responsibility, this thankless leadership. I was never able to convince Mildred to comply, and I never knew exactly where she'd gone. The last phase of my "leadership" duty, therefore, was to scour the neighborhood, knocking on door after door and calling out, "Is Mildred here?" until I found her and escorted her home.

Once home, Sonja and I watched Mildred getting a spanking, forever wishing we could have convinced her to avoid that fate. The final straw was that after the spanking, Mildred's tears dried instantly. Feeling no remorse, she resumed her happy-go-lucky life.

I felt like a failed leader. I was drained and distraught.

I realize now, of course, that I was not a failed leader. I was a little girl. Being the big sister is a heavy responsibility, but children cannot be expected to perform the role of adult parents in all instances. When a family's circumstances make it unavoidable, however, children experience this as overwhelming. Since those years, I have stepped forward to lead many groups and activities, and I have sometimes become a leader in unexpected situations. I've now come to believe that we each have within us an inner leader; and while mine was perhaps called upon at too young an age, nonetheless my mother unwittingly helped me identify and develop my inner leader early in life. Honoring the call to lead gives a deep satisfaction that can enhance and heighten our happiness, and I am grateful for my early lessons.

Have you ever thought of yourself as a leader? If you're like most people, you probably haven't. We tend to think of a stereotypical leader as the head of a corporation, organization, or military command.

When I urge you to honor your inner leader, I'm not suggesting that you must be a CEO, a celebrity, the founder of a nonprofit organization, or the organizer of a humanitarian movement. What I am suggesting is that there is a leader within each of us, and a leader who is waiting to be honored.

So who is it you're leading?

First, you are leading yourself. The goals you set for yourself not only bring results to you but also influence and impact others in your life. Your happiness depends on your motivation and determination to go after and achieve your goals. That makes being a leader of yourself one of your most important roles.

Second, even though you don't realize or notice it, someone may already be following your lead. Whether you're single or married, an employee or the boss, or the neighbor quietly tending her garden each day, someone is being influenced by what you say and do.

Don't let this scare you! There is one way to ensure that you are a good leader of yourself and others: *Follow your higher calling*. When you feel that inner tug to do good or to do the right thing—*respond to it*. I believe that each of us has a life purpose, a passion that, if we tap into it, will give us lasting happiness and lead us to make a positive difference in the world.

What do leaders look like?

When I was still teaching college, on the first day of each new semester, I always scanned my classes to see if I could spot the class leaders. These students would be the ones who would take a key role in the personality and atmosphere of the class. They would find new confidence as they mastered the analytical skills they would develop and would, in turn, help me enlighten and inspire the rest of the class.

I could never tell just by looking at them, but when I broke the class into random groups of five students each to analyze an essay, a leader always emerged without any help from me. Usually the group would chit-chat nervously for a moment or two, and then one of them would take charge and get the group started on the task at hand.

Leaders are sometimes difficult to spot at first glance.

Mother Teresa, for example, was a frail nun who never set out to be a leader or a celebrity. Although the terms *celebrity* and *leader* are not the same, many leaders are catapulted to celebrity status in the public mind, based on their visibility and accomplishments.

Mother Teresa was so unconcerned with the details of her life that her birthday was frequently misreported. But when she saw the almost overwhelming poverty in India, which was not her native country, she was moved to help the poor and disenfranchised there. Her passion and selfless work resonated around the world and drew support from all of us. Without benefit of board meetings, corporate reports, or computer analyses, she became recognized around the world because she saw a need and worked to meet it.

Let me tell you about an unassuming couple, Lewis and Edna Cole, whom I met in 1958 on what seemed like a typical Sunday at the Central Baptist Church in St. Louis. The sermon was delivered, scriptures were referenced and quoted, and a flyer was distributed as we left the sanctuary. There was no way that I or anyone else could have known the significance of that day. The flyer was directed at teenagers. It was an invitation.

Teenagers from fourteen to seventeen were invited to attend the first meeting of a new youth group. As I remember it, the theme was "bringing in the harvest." The flyer promised activities, food, and fun. All I could think was that this church-sanctioned group would surely win my mother's approval and give me an opportunity to inspect boys close up. It was definitely a win-win situation. At age thirteen, I was a year too young, but I knew I could make a convincing argument for why I should be admitted. I succeeded and was able to join our new youth group, the Central Youth Council, later known as the CYC.

Lewis and Edna, the young couple who'd agreed to lead the group, seemed far too timid and soft-spoken to corral the thirty rambunctious teenagers who showed up for that first meeting.

Edna Cole, especially, didn't seem to look like a leader. She was petite, weighed barely one hundred pounds, and spoke in a high-pitched, stammering voice. But she was determined and persistent. What she lacked in physical size, she made up for in vision and stick-to-it-iveness.

Louis was of average height and slender build. He was easy going and soft spoken. When he stood up and placed his index finger on his cheek, we stopped our chatter and listened. We knew he was about to give us his final word on whatever issue we had been vigorously debating.

As typical teenagers, we tried to pull a few fast ones on them, but we never got very far. Without getting angry or wringing anyone's neck, they always kept control of the group so we could complete our activities. Under the guidance of Edna and Louis, we teens produced and acted in some spectacular dramatic productions, fundraisers, and other events. And we deepened our spiritual belief along the way.

Not only did Edna help shape our teenage lives, but her influence continues to shape our adult lives. Through the years she served as the matriarch of the CYC, she kept us informed of each other's whereabouts.

In November of 2007, fifty years after our group began, we gathered in St. Louis for a reunion. During this weekend, we got to tell the Coles in person what their lives had meant to us. As a group, we finally shared our deep gratitude, love, and appreciation for Mr. and Mrs. Cole, who had guided us through the treacherous waters of adolescence.

Our fifty-year reunion began Friday evening with a kickoff party. We greeted each other and joked around as if no years had passed at all. As usual, the Coles observed us quietly, chuckling now and then at our antics. While a videographer recorded our conversations and huddles, Mrs. Cole quietly pulled out a scrapbook and handed it to one of the members of the CYC. Filled with grand pictures of us dressed in our formal gowns and tuxedos at CYC Coronations, the scrapbook made its way around the room. Gasps and exclamations abounded. "Is that me?" "Look at you!" "Wow, you were handsome!" "I still am!" How we fought back the tears, I don't know. There was so much joy being together again.

Saturday's celebration began with brunch. We made our way around the buffet with the same gusto we'd brought to the many lunches and dinners at CYC parties and events when we were young. During that meal, we came up with the idea of creating a musical tribute to the Coles by writing new lyrics to the song "Wind Beneath My Wings."

At the party that Saturday night, we serenaded the Coles with our musical tribute. They truly had been the "Wind Beneath Our Wings." On Sunday, we worshipped and had communion together at our childhood church, after which we announced the Lewis and Edna Cole Scholarship, which was awarded to a college-bound high school graduate every June beginning in 2008.

Lewis and Edna have passed away now. But even as we become senior citizens, the impact they made on us is still strong.

What is a leader?

First, let's dispel a few myths.

Myth #1: Leaders are born. This antiquated notion has traditionally helped ensure that leaders came from the aristocracy, thereby blocking the average person from ever having the chance to become a leader. This system subjected the world to some weak and evil aristocrats who either grabbed leadership or just let it happen to them. Some of them undoubtedly would have preferred not to be forced into leadership.

Myth #2: Leaders must have certain traits. A few traits thought to indicate leadership ability are creativity, determination, assertiveness, self-confidence, and a fluent speaking ability. While leaders certainly have these and many other admirable traits, experts can't seem to agree on precisely what the required traits are.

Myth #3: Leaders are heads of organizations, corporations, and countries. You don't have to be the head of an organization or a company to be a leader. Leaders have emerged in some of the most unlikely places and some of the most unexpected times. Inventors tinkering in their garages looking for a better way to communicate or college students who devise a way for students to connect with each other all can go on to become leaders. And many have done so.

> *Some are born great, some achieve greatness,*
> *and some have greatness thrust upon them.*
> —Shakespeare, *Twelfth Night* (Act II, Sc. 5)

Leaders can emerge in unlikely times and places

When Rosa Parks refused to surrender her bus seat to a white passenger, as was the law in Montgomery, Alabama, on December 1, 1955, she was not asserting herself as a leader. As a matter of fact, because she had once had a negative encounter with James Blake, the driver of the bus that day, she has reported that she would not even have gotten on his bus if she'd noticed he was the driver.

Of course, Parks was no stranger to the struggles faced by blacks in the South. As a long-time member and secretary of the Montgomery chapter of the National Association for the Advancement of Colored People (NAACP), she was a political activist before she got on the bus. She had also recently attended a workshop for social and economic justice at Tennessee's Highlander Folk School.

Once on Blake's bus, however, she took a seat in the front row of the approved section for African Americans. A white man was left standing when the "whites-only" section filled up. When the driver demanded that Parks and three others in the row leave their seats to make room for the white passenger, the other three people complied.

Rosa Parks refused, even though she clearly knew the possible consequences. Many black people had been whipped and even lynched for less.

Rosa Parks' quiet courage, which led to her arrest and a fine for violating a city ordinance, led to the thirteen-month-long Montgomery Bus Boycott led by Martin Luther King and thrust her to the forefront of a wave of protest that rippled across America. It eventually led to the end of legal segregation in America. Her refusal to give up her seat changed the course of history.

Parks paid dearly for her bravery. Within weeks after the boycott, she lost her department store job. During and after the boycott, she received hostile phone calls and death threats. Eventually, she and her husband moved to Detroit, Michigan, where she worked for many years as administrative aide for Congressman John Conyers, Jr.

When Rosa Parks died in 2005 at the age of ninety-two, she became the first woman in history to rest in state at the U.S. Capitol. This was an honor previously reserved for Presidents of the United States.

Rosa Parks was asked many times why she didn't yield her seat on the bus. It has been reported that she said, "My feet were tired," but that isn't exactly what happened. On June 2, 1995, in Williamsburg, Virginia, when Rosa Parks was interviewed by the Academy of Achievement, she said:

> I made up my mind that I would not give in any longer to legally imposed racial segregation. I don't remember feeling... anger, but I did feel determined to take this as an opportunity to let it be known that I did not want to be treated in that manner and that people have endured it far too long. However, I did not have at the moment of my arrest any idea of how the people would react.

For her role in the civil rights movement, President Clinton presented Rosa Parks with the Presidential

Medal of Freedom in 1996. In 1999, she received a Congressional Gold Medal.

When things get tough, brace for impact

Every year, an individual of distinction is selected to be the Grand Marshal of the Tournament of Roses Parade in Pasadena, California. On January 1, 2010, the Grand Marshal of the 121st Parade was Chesley Burnett "Sully" Sullenberger III. He was the celebrated airline pilot and hero who had landed U.S. Airways Flight 1549 in the icy waters of the Hudson River in New York in January 2009, saving the lives of 155 passengers and crew.

Captain Sullenberger's ride in the Rose Bowl Parade, leading a line of flower-bedecked floats, was, according to his comment to the press, "a lot more fun and stress-free" than safely landing his crippled passenger jet in full view of New Yorkers gathered near the river. (In one of many interviews, Captain Sullenberger admitted that he had always wanted to see the Rose Bowl Parade in person.)

What made Captain Sullenberger an overnight hero was not just that he made a successful landing and averted a disaster. He is celebrated because when faced with a startling dilemma, he assessed the situation, made a decision, and braced himself and his crew for the impact he could not avoid. But thanks to his skill, the jet landed on the river and did not sink. It could have been very different, of course, but Captain Sullenberger did not ponder the problem or hesitate to take action. That's what saved lives.

Most of us will never be faced with a heart-pounding crisis like the one that gripped Captain Sullenberger that day, but we will all be faced with some situations that require us to brace for impact.

When Faced with a Crisis, Use What You Know

On August 20, 2013, Antoinette Tuff, an elementary school clerk at the Ronald E. McNair Discovery Learning Academy in Atlanta, Georgia, talked down a gunman who was set on taking his own life and the lives of as many others as he could. During news interviews afterward, Ms. Tuff admitted that she was scared inside, but her experience of divorce after a thirty-three-year marriage, a contemplated suicide, and coping with a child suffering from multiple disabilities, gave her courage. She especially thought of the 800 students at the school that day who were cowering in their classrooms.

As Ms. Tuff faced this troubled gunman alone in the school office, she thought of her own son and felt compassion and empathy for the young man with the gun. As she began speaking, he began listening. She shared her own struggles with him and reassured him that he could get past this. She especially reminded the would-be mass murderer that although shots had been fired, no one had been killed yet. If he gave himself up, she said, he could get help. Her pastor's recent sermons on anchoring (a focusing and decision-making technique) echoed in her mind, and she had also completed recent training for dealing with hostile situations. She used what she'd learned to save the lives of the children in the school.

Most of you are not faced with situations as dramatic and far-reaching as those faced by Parks, Sullenberger, and Tuff. But your crises can nonetheless feel devastating. You may have lost your job, your life savings, or your hope. To survive, you must find inner strength and take positive action to lead yourself through the crisis. Here's what to do:

- Assess your situation.
- Determine what you can do right now.
- Use the tools and resources that can help you.
- Brace for impact.
- Take bold action.

You may never be called upon to save a nation or a planeload of people or talk down a gunman, but if you can brace for the impact of your personal adversity, you can emerge successful.

> *There are three rules for creating good leaders. Unfortunately, no one knows what they are.*
>
> —W. Somerset Maugham

You may be wondering why I'm discussing leaders and leadership in a book about creating happiness. Perhaps you have never thought about being a leader or aspired to be one. I'm asking you now to accept the fact that the potential for leadership is within us all.

Acknowledging and releasing this potential will bring you lasting happiness, even if the situation that brought it out was unpleasant.

Someday you, like Rosa Parks, may find yourself unwilling to put up with unfair treatment or you may feel compelled to speak up for what's right. You may feel a strong need to take a stand, and take action that will bring about positive change.

It's your responsibility and your duty to share your leadership talents with the world. That's why it's important to understand that a leader doesn't have to be at the top of a large corporation or institution. Each of us, no matter where we stand in the pecking order, has a leadership role to play in our daily lives at home and at work.

Once we move beyond the idea that leaders possess certain inborn traits, we can see leaders based on *what they do* in various situations. We can also become comfortable with the truth that there is a leader in each of us. With this in mind, I favor this definition of a leader:

> You are a leader if you influence others to accomplish a goal and direct them in ways to proceed smoothly, directly, and willingly. The very first person you influence is yourself.

What sets leaders apart from the rest of us is their behavior

- The U.S. Army says a leader must "Be, Know, and Do."
- The New York Fire Department says a leader is "first in, last out."
- Lee Iacocca says a leader picks good people and sets the right priorities.
- Jesse Jackson says, "Leadership has a harder job to do than just choose sides. It must bring sides together."
- E. M. Kelly says, "The difference between a boss and a leader: a boss says, 'Go!'- a leader says, 'Let's go!'"
- Brenda Barnes, former CEO of Sara Lee, who managed a staff of 52,000 employees, says a good leader creates an environment where everyone brings his or her best talent to the fore and best ability to work every day.

The leader who exercises power with honor will work from the inside out, starting with himself.

—Blaine Lee

You are indeed a leader, so ask yourself if and how you bring out the best in others. Are you willing to step forward to do the right thing, even if you're usually the quiet one? Are you able to set your own priorities and go after your own goals?

Let's take a closer look at the behaviors exhibited by leaders:

A LEADER LOOKS AHEAD

Leaders have a vision of *what can be*, not just an observation of *what is*. Leaders can look at an open plain and see a city, look at a block of clay and see a statue, look at a blank sheet of paper and see a novel or a concerto.

Although many leaders were not trained to be leaders, they are able to see ahead. Some leaders were labeled as heretics and lunatics before they found success. Consider the following so-called heretics and lunatics.

- Can man fly? The Wright Brothers thought so. They invented the airplane.
- Can we talk to someone across town or the world? Alexander Graham Bell thought so. He invented the telephone.
- Can we look at the heavens and predict the weather for a year? A number of people believed so. Most notably were Benjamin Franklin who published Poor Richard's Almanack from 1732 to1758 and Benjamin Banneker, a descendant of slaves, who published the Farmer's Almanac between 1792 and 1797.
- Can a woman lead a military victory? Joan of Arc thought so. Acting under divine guidance, she cropped her hair and disguised herself as a man. Then she led the French army to victory over the

English in the Hundred Years War. The English army captured her, however, and accused her of witchcraft. Then they burned her at the stake for violating a biblical injunction against women dressing as men.

A LEADER EDUCATES HERSELF

Leaders are always learning by reading and attending classes and trainings. My mother repeated this Persian proverb so frequently that it still echoes in my mind today:

He who knows not and knows not he knows not: He is a fool—shun him.
He who knows not and knows he knows not: He is simple—teach him.
He who knows and knows not he knows: He is asleep—wake him.
He who knows and knows he knows: He is wise—follow him

A LEADER ASSESSES AND PRIORITIZES

Like Sullenberger and Tuff, leaders are often called upon to survey a situation and decide, sometimes very quickly, what steps need to be taken to resolve that situation.

To be able to assess a situation, it's important to know yourself. Be comfortable with your strengths, and be willing to admit your weaknesses. Some people get to know themselves by journaling, practicing self-care, and not trying to fit in all the time. They learn to be comfortable with their own thoughts and decisions, even when those thoughts and decisions are unpopular. They work on being flexible and being open to different ways of approaching situations.

> *Nothing so conclusively proves a man's ability to lead others as what he does from day to day to lead himself.*
>
> —Thomas J. Watson
> Founder of IBM

A LEADER DELEGATES

Leaders are able to break goals down into manageable pieces and assign those pieces to people who can get the job done. This doesn't mean barking orders. It means empowering others to get things done by respecting their ideas and creating an encouraging, inclusive, and inspiring work environment.

Delegating does not mean dumping work on others, either. It means allowing people to complete tasks that contribute to the goals of the group.

Trying to go it alone, whether going after your personal goals or those of a business, is asking for burnout. A great leader who gets help from others not only gets the job done but also bolsters the pride and satisfaction of the other people who have been part of a successful endeavor.

A LEADER EMPATHIZES WITH OTHERS

One of the most important characteristics of leaders is their ability to empathize. This means *listening to the needs of others* and creating an environment where they feel free to express their feelings. It means maintaining an open door policy so employees, family, and friends feel comfortable discussing problems and other issues early on.

According to *USA Today*, 50 percent of workers hate their jobs (Grant, 2013). They don't just want pay increases, though. While it's commonly thought that job dissatisfaction is primarily about salaries, people want more than pay increases. People want:

- Tools and systems to do their jobs
- A work role that allows them to grow
- Coworkers who pull their own weight
- Recognition for a job well done
- Fair and equal treatment
- Stimulating work tasks

It's believed that one third of employees don't feel respected by their supervisors. Some bosses are even accused of treating employees like children or criminals. In 1983, a series of murders by U.S. postal workers against their supervisors, coworkers, the police, and the general public filled the news. The cause for these rampages was given as workplace rage stemming from numerous personal and workplace problems. Even though this type of violence erupted in many work settings, the term "going postal" entered our common vocabulary to refer to bloodshed occurring in the workplace as a result of rage.

After these incidents, surviving employees reported that those who had gone postal were enraged over being fired or being assigned what they saw as unfair workloads. But sometimes the perpetrators had heard their bosses speaking in demeaning and cruel ways to or about them and others.

As a leader in your own life, on your job, or in your family, you must *be sensitive to the feelings and concerns of others*. This responsibility is not to be taken lightly. While we are not responsible for the mental and personal problems that people bring to a job or into a relationship, we certainly are responsible for how we interact with them in conversation and behavior.

Once at the community college where I taught, a teacher leaving class was attacked by the husband of one of her students. I was appalled. I couldn't imagine what had provoked such an attack. The teacher taught English as a Second Language to a diverse group of adults of varied nationalities and from many countries. I later learned that she routinely made insensitive and condescending comments to and about the students and their cultures. Her rude behavior does not, however, justify the broken arm she sustained in the attack by an angry husband who believed he was protecting his wife's honor. As leader of the class, the teacher had made poor choices when she insulted her students. She let her class down by failing to create a welcoming and encouraging environment.

A LEADER ROCKS THE BOAT

A leader is willing to upset the status quo to keep the company, group, club, or organization moving toward its vision. Good leaders don't rock the boat just to be annoying, though. Because of their vision for the organization, they can see beyond the present and are willing to take risks to get there. Their ideas will often be opposed by others who are comfortable with the way things are. That's why they have to rock the boat. It gets people's attention.

When Rosa Parks refused to give up her seat, she was definitely rocking the boat. She even broke the law. It was not her intent to start a movement, but she saw beyond the oppression of black people and recognized that she could no longer go along with an unfair law.

There will come a time in your life when your values and vision are out of sync with society's status quo or when you are increasingly opposed to common practices. During these times, your happiness depends on your honoring your inner leader. Don't discredit your inner leader by ignoring it.

I hope the tips and stories I've shared in this chapter give you the courage to step forward to make a positive difference in your life and in the world. For example, if you don't like reality TV and deeply believe that it damages our culture, you certainly can't insist that other viewers and TV producers conform to your preferences. But you can gather input from others in your community or like-minded people, and you can find research and gather data that support your viewpoint. Then you can make a formal complaint to those who can do something about TV programming. You can take the lead in bringing about legislation or other positive change in programming.

> Color yourself *powerful* by wearing black. Black is timeless and versatile. It can convey authority when worn in a business setting, but it can also represent humility and respect, as when worn by priests and nuns.
>
> Wear too much black, however, and you run the risk of appearing scary, evil, or villainous. If your intent is to embrace the dark side, promote an alternative lifestyle, or align with punk, goth, glam rock, and other subcultures, then all black is the color for you.

Summary

There's a leader lurking inside you! Your inner leader might not manage a corporation or negotiate with foreign powers, but he or she is still a leader. The leader in you might step forward to snatch a child from the path of a speeding car or organize the passengers on an airplane to thwart the efforts of a group of terrorists intent on destroying a building in Washington, DC. Or your leader may step forward to rescue a stranded family clinging to the roof of their sinking home during a flood. While we think of these folks as heroes because they risked their lives to do something extraordinary, they are also leaders because they took control of a situation and inspired us by their selflessness, courage, decisive, and fast action.

A leader is always somewhat heroic, even when his actions are not dramatic. She may be a committee member who bravely stands alone to oppose an issue others are afraid to support. By honoring and respecting her own inner leader, she earns the respect of coworkers who are too intimidated to reveal their true viewpoints.

Happiness Flashback

I once decided to paint the living room, dining room, kitchen, and family room all bright yellow. When I asked Sonya, my second daughter, how she liked the new color, she said, "I feel like I'm sitting in a jar of mustard."

Chapter 10

Connecting the Dots

It was a few months before my high school graduation when newly elected President John F. Kennedy officially launched the Peace Corps and challenged young Americans to devote two years of their lives to help with various projects in countries of the developing world. I was seventeen when I was accepted to serve and assigned to Addis Ababa, Ethiopia. As I leafed through the papers that explained in detail how to prepare for my assignment and saw how much I needed to do to get ready to be transported to a country and lifestyle so different from my own, I became light-headed.

Excited and scared at the same time, I consulted one of my mother's favorite beauty shop customers, Mrs. Roberts. She was an English teacher and had always encouraged me in my early academic accomplishments, from learning to read to writing poetry to meeting other milestones in school. My mother admired Mrs. Roberts' independence and her flair for living, which were reflected in her sophisticated manner of speaking, her elegant attire, and her world travels. (I still have a souvenir she brought me from the Holy Land, a white cotton handkerchief with "Jerusalem" embroidered in red.)

Many things about Mrs. Roberts fascinated me. Her name was unique: Aucetralia. She spoke with measured certainty when giving advice, and she shared stories and jokes skillfully. I was amazed that she could have such a very light complexion and straight hair and still be African American. She was often mistaken for a Caucasian.

Mrs. Roberts had a bi-monthly hair appointment with my mother, and I always looked forward to her visits. My mother's patrons didn't just come for the hairstyles. They often came early or stayed after their appointments to chat, catch up on gossip, and exchange advice. Some of these women even helped my mom with household chores like ironing. Others, like Mrs. Roberts, always drew me into the conversation by inquiring about my progress in school and encouraging my latest poems, compositions, or other writing.

When I told Mrs. Roberts I had volunteered for the Peace Corps, she praised my desire to do good in the world. To my surprise, however, she also discouraged me from devoting two years of my life to this endeavor. In her mind, she said, those two years would be better spent pursuing my college goals and getting into my chosen career faster. She pointed out that I already knew what it was like to live in a poor neighborhood. She said that finishing college would open the door for me to create a life I hadn't experienced before.

Maybe I took her advice because it meant staying in my comfort zone on the college track. Whatever the reason, I abandoned my plan to go into the Peace Corps and never returned the paperwork.

It was the first time I remember changing my mind about something without caring whether my mother agreed or not.

I have only realized now, decades later, how much influence those conversations and encounters with Mrs. Roberts had on my life choices. Not only did I take her advice about not entering the Peace Corps, but as soon as I entered college, I also joined the same sorority she was a member of, became an English teacher as she was, and set a goal to travel the world as she had done.

Although you are influenced by the people you meet, the experiences you have, and even by the failures you encounter, it's unlikely that you can pinpoint exactly what event or idea leads to your choices. Choices and reasons for choosing are intricately intertwined. And yet, as I did, you do connect ideas to decide on your next steps.

How do we connect the dots?

None of us can be sure where our choices in the present will eventually lead us.

- When I decided to go to college after high school graduation instead of joining the Peace Corps, I couldn't know if that was the right decision.
- When we arrived in California too late for me to enroll in UCLA as I had planned, to continue my teacher preparation, I enrolled in Los Angeles City College and spent a glorious year majoring in Theater Arts instead. Upon completion of that year, I enrolled in the University of Southern California and used all those drama units as my minor.
- When I accepted a doctoral grant that required me to quit my full-time teaching position and become a full-time student for four years, there was no way to know if our young family's lifestyle could survive the big drop in our income.

Scary though these choices may have appeared to outsiders, they were not random. I had faith that they were right for me. Each misstep gave me information to help with the next step, and each success gave me confidence to move forward.

Measure to get feedback

While we're often advised to set goals, we can't improve what we don't measure. That's why the first step in changing our eating habits, for example, whether for health or weight loss, is to keep a record of what we're currently eating, weigh ourselves, and note physical activity and other relevant information. It's only when we get feedback via measuring what we are currently doing that we can decide what step to take next.

To move forward in life, we must set a destination. But we must also identify our starting point.

James Clear, an entrepreneur, weightlifter, and travel photographer, suggested that we measure backward. This means we should keep track of what we've done in our recent past in order to plan what to do in our future. In his business and personal life, for example, Clear keeps a record of what he has accomplished before starting the current week's activities. He chronicled in his blog post how he increased his workouts by making small increases. In his business and his physical fitness, he measures backwards to decide on his next move. (http://jamesclear.com/measure-backward)

Keeping track of progress as we plan future steps has an added benefit. Small achievements add to your sense of accomplishment and thereby boost your happiness.

WHAT ABOUT THOSE FAILURES AND SETBACKS?

Imagine beams of sunshine pouring through your bedroom window and awakening you. You unfold your arms into a satisfying stretch and throw back the sheets. You roll out of bed and spring to your feet, looking forward to a wonderful day.

You're sure you aced the interview a few days ago. But later that morning, when you open the envelope from your prospective employer, you learn you didn't get the job.

Instead of deciding what to wear on your first day at the new job, you're going to spend another day job hunting. And you've got to figure out (again) how to stretch the few dollars left in your bank account.

> *Every adversity, every failure, every heartache carries with it the seed of an equal or greater benefit.*
>
> —Napoleon Hill

We all encounter adversity, failure, and setbacks, no matter how hard we plan or try to avoid them. Our challenge is to handle them well until we manifest the good outcome we want.

But this is easier said than done because, as humans, we love to look in all the wrong places for solutions.

Is your solution a mask or a cure?

When we get a headache, we search for an aspirin. When we spot a blemish, we apply an ointment. And when someone rejects us, we are tempted to lash out at them or spend time hating them. Or getting even.

When we try to solve what we see as a problem using an external solution, we're engaging in an exercise in futility.

Consider the common cold. We've heard many times that there is no cure, and yet we spend millions on so-called cures. Along with the over-the-counter medications, we get prescriptions from our doctor and advice to drink liquids and get plenty of rest. And when the cold runs its course, it goes away. All the cure activities we engaged in for several days just kept us busy masking the symptoms. We didn't cure the cold. Recovery was just a matter of time.

We have a choice about how we view everything that happens in our lives.

Is this a major setback or a divine setup?

When we don't ace that job interview or maybe aren't selected for the interview, we may decide it's a setback. But it may be a divine setup for a better job. When we miss a plane, we may decide it's a setback that delays our vacation or makes us late for a meeting. Yet it may be another divine setup that prevents us from getting on a plane that crashes. Or it makes us available for a more positive event or relationship.

The next time something happens that you would normally see as a setback, pause and think of another way to look at it.

Chances are it isn't the end of the world. Consider that a higher power, or whatever power you believe in, is at work putting you in a situation that will lead you in a better direction than you expected.

The next time you perceive something as a setback, don't spend time resenting it or replaying it in your head as if you could change it. Look for the lesson, the blessing, or the seed of a surprising benefit. Connect those dots!

Look not at the days gone by with a forlorn heart. They were simply the dots we can now connect with our present, to help us draw the outline of a beautiful tomorrow.

—Dodinsky, *In the Garden of Thoughts*

Maybe you want to make positive changes in your life, but you are not sure where to begin. Some of what I've shared in the previous chapters may encourage you to make significant changes. Other ideas and experiences may have convinced you to stay on your chosen path and keep working to reach the goals you have already set. The only place you can begin to make changes is where you are now. The only person who knows what is right for you is you.

I hope you've gotten the message that there is no one-size-fits-all right or wrong way to create the life you want. When you hear about a new option, examine your mind and heart to see what resonates with you. Then take one step at a time as you give yourself permission to change your mind and your direction as you go.

How do you decide what path to follow?

It wasn't my intention to give contradictory advice, but it could have happened. Well-intentioned friends, parents, books, and leaders frequently give us conflicting advice, but we don't notice the contradictions unless we set the choices and words of advice side by side and look at them more closely. When we get fuzzy advice like "Follow your dream," it can just confuse us.

Here are some of my favorite bits of fuzzy advice.

1. Finish college, it's the best investment in your future.
2. A traditional four-year college degree is a terrible investment.
3. Absence makes the heart grow fonder.
4. Out of sight, out of mind.
5. Look before you leap.
6. He who hesitates is lost.
7. It's better to be safe than sorry.
8. Nothing ventured, nothing gained.
9. Take a chance and venture far from shore.
10. *Bloom where you're planted.*

When you encounter contradictory advice, stop, listen carefully, and then consider the background and the motives of the speaker. Consult people you trust. Treat the advice as feedback and opinion, but also think about how it applies to your life. Then make up your own mind and decide your own course of action.

And once you're clear on what's right for you, be indifferent to what others think.

Five ways to connect the dots to create your version of happiness

1. *Measure advice against your own value system and goals.*

> "Take Criminology 101," one of my college friends advised me when we were choosing classes for the last semester of our junior year.
>
> "Criminology 101? Why?" I didn't understand why this was a good idea. "That's totally unrelated to my major."
>
> "That doesn't matter," my friend said with a straight face. "It's an easy *A* and will raise your GPA."

It's common for college friends to recommend teachers, but taking a class that didn't interest me didn't make sense to me, even as an elective.

I also had a much more compelling reason to disregard her advice.

I was fortunate to have attended my first two years of college practically for free. I'd been awarded a scholarship to my hometown teacher's college my freshman year, and when my family moved to California during my sophomore year, I attended a community college at a time when there was no tuition. I always worked part-time jobs to pay for my own books and incidentals.

But my junior year was different. I wanted to transfer to the University of Southern California, where tuition was (and still is) formidable. Without knowing what the tuition would cost, my mother was eager for me to attend because the campus was walking distance from my house and she had heard from neighbors that it was a prestigious school. Since she was working full-time and going to night school to earn her California cosmetology license, she assigned me the task of walking over to the campus to find out the registration procedure and tuition.

I was mesmerized by the university atmosphere. The cobblestone streets, the brick buildings, and the impressive landscaping were exactly what I felt a university should look like. But when I went home with a fistful of paperwork and the schedule of classes, I was reluctant to reveal the tuition cost. I was sure my hope of attending USC would be dashed in its infancy.

"How much is tuition?" my mother asked that evening. She got to the point right away.

"It's $36 per unit," I gulped, then quickly added, "but there's a flat fee for a full-time load."

Thirty-six dollars a unit seemed like a fortune to me in 1963.

"Okay," my mother said slowly as she began processing this news and doing multiplication in her head. "When do you need to pay it?"

As I gave her the details, I could see that she was already calculating how she would manage this huge but important investment. I don't think financial aid existed at the time. At least we hadn't heard of it.

After what seemed like a long time, she said, "I'll see what I can do."

I silently rejoiced because this was my mother's way of saying that she was going to make this happen.

The next day, I walked the six blocks from our house, taking a shortcut across Exposition Park, and entered the south side of the campus clutching $600 in cash to pay for the first semester of my junior year at USC.

As she folded the bills carefully and watched me put the money in my pocket, my mother had given me very clear instructions:

> Here's the money for your first semester. As soon as you get enrolled and start classes, find out if you can get a scholarship or a loan to pay for the rest of the way.
>
> Don't tell your grandfather how much it cost! He won't understand. He thinks girls should just get married and have babies.

I did as she told me. I found a way to pay for the rest of my education on my own, and I also never discussed my tuition with my grandfather. During the first semester of my junior year, I found a loan that paid for the rest of my bachelor's degree and teaching credential that I didn't have to start repaying until I began teaching. For each year that I taught, part of my loan was forgiven. I paid it off in five years.

So now you see why I scoffed at my classmate's suggestion that I take a class I didn't need. I would never have wasted my mother's money like that.

2. *Dedicate yourself to loving, supporting, and being true to yourself.*

> *Don't put the key to your happiness in someone else's pocket.*
>
> —Unknown

As I neared my forty-fifth birthday, I began to think about how I wanted to celebrate. Perhaps I'd go out to my favorite restaurant, attend a special theater performance, or invite a few friends over for cake and ice cream. These were my default celebrations.

Then I began to recall the themed birthday parties I had given my four children over the years—marionette theater, magic show, skating party, ice cream parlor, and many others. The celebrations I had given myself were fun, but unremarkable by comparison.

That's when it occurred to me that I had never given myself a themed party. As a matter of fact, I couldn't remember ever having a special birthday party in my lifetime. Sure, my mother always celebrated our childhood birthdays with a cake and ice cream and invited neighborhood friends, but now I longed for a special celebration. It was a turning point. I decided to give myself exactly the party I wanted without concern for approval from others.

My mind went into high gear as I explored what kind of themed birthday party I would most enjoy. As I thought about the friends I would invite, I recalled how most of my girlfriends came to events alone because their husbands didn't want to come along. That's when I decided to give a girls-only party. That way, the husbands and boyfriends wouldn't have to concoct excuses for not attending. Since they wouldn't be invited, they would be off the hook.

My girls-only party now began to take shape. Since we were all adults, I thought it would be a hoot to make it X-rated. One of my friends told me her cousin's boyfriend, a local fireman, performed as a stripper for parties on the weekends, so I hired him. He was a great dancer and cleared it with me beforehand how far down to strip. I told him he could strip down to the thong—I didn't want any of my girlfriends to pass out, even though he was qualified to give CPR just in case. I'm sure my party was tame by comparison to some X-rated parties, but since my friends were mostly sedate educators like me, I knew it would be hilarious to watch their reactions and interactions. Another friend referred me to a numerologist to do readings for each guest. I hired him, too.

Since I worked at a college, I knew exactly where the X-rated stores were located. That's where I went to buy games and party favors. We played several games, but the most hilarious one was a game like Pin the Tail on the Donkey except it was Pin the Condom on the Penis of a very buff guy on a wall poster. We laughed so hard during this game because here we were middle-aged married ladies who, once blindfolded, could not hit our mark. Not one of us pinned our condom near the target.

Fortunately I also thought to hire a professional photographer to capture memorable shots of this first of my many themed parties.

Some friends were shocked and amazed that I would put together what they considered a bold and risqué party. Perhaps you are, too. That's okay. You can create the celebrations of life events that have meaning for you.

Since then, I've celebrated my birthdays with many themes: a western, complete with costumes (I was Mae West) and square dancing. A catered fiesta. A jazz club. A chili cook-off.

At my chili cook-off birthday party, I promised to publish the first-place winner's recipe in this book. The chili submitted by my friend Nancy K. Strasser won first place, so here is her recipe.

Nancy's Chili Con Carne

Chile con carne, the official dish of the State of Texas, is an American invention, not a Mexican dish, as many people think. It is popular in restaurants and home parties and is a favorite at cook-offs. Aficionados disagree about whether proper chili con carne has beans, meat, and/or tomatoes. Nancy used all three of these ingredients.

¾ teaspoon salt
1 pound lean ground beef
1 medium-size onion, chopped
1 can (14 oz.) pear-shaped tomatoes
1 large can (1 lb. 11 oz.) red kidney beans
1½ teaspoons chili powder
1 teaspoon oregano leaves, crumbled
½ teaspoon ground cumin seed
Avocado slices
¼ cup coarsely chopped fresh coriander (cilantro)

Put a frying pan over medium high and heat the salt. Crumble ground beef into skillet and cook, stirring, until browned. Add chopped onion and cook until limp. Strain off any fat. Stir in tomatoes and kidney beans, along with their liquids. Add chili powder, oregano, and cumin. Simmer in the pan uncovered and break up the tomatoes while stirring occasionally for about 1 hour and 30 minutes until the chili thickens slightly. Add the avocado slices and coriander to garnish. Makes about four servings.

Even though some folks react with surprise that I would give myself these themed parties, I am not deterred. I decided that the best way to get the party you want is to give it yourself, and, after all, I deserve to celebrate in my own way.

I am not suggesting you celebrate your birthday with themed parties as I did. This is not at all about birthday parties or any particular celebrations.

I'm urging you to love and support yourself by choosing activities and goals that are true to you. You may have longed to try sky diving, to learn to ice skate, to write a book, or rescue abandoned pets. There are an infinite number of choices.

Once you discover what you enjoy, don't hold back for fear of what others may think. And please don't feel guilty for wanting the things you want. Or for getting them. Connect the dots of your life experiences that lead to the choices that give you joy and fulfillment.

Keep the key to your happiness in your possession.

3. ***Create a whole life.*** People who are fond of reading self-help books sometimes make the mistake of letting the reading of the book substitute for taking action. It's easy to feel good as you read about things other people have faced and how those other people overcame their obstacles. But it's downright scary to put down that book and actually take action in your own life.

Susan Jeffers (1987) wrote one of the best-selling self-help books of all time. Originally published in 1987, it is still in Amazon's Top 100 Paid books. When I discovered this book, I had closed my private tutoring program and separated from my husband. I was still raising my four children and holding down four part-time jobs to pay the bills while I eagerly looked for a new full-time job, or even new career if necessary.

One night after a class I taught at a local community college ended, one of my students recommended Jeffers' book. I don't know how she knew I needed it, but she was absolutely right. For a few years, I read it every year. It became my bible and propelled me forward through transitions. It helped me connect the dots in my life.

Two powerful concepts in Jeffers' book jolted me into action:

- I was never going to wake up fearless one morning. But I could move forward in spite of my fear, step into what I wanted even if it scared me, and come out successful on the other side. Or I could remain stuck, waiting for that day of fearlessness that would never come.
- It was up to me to choose activities and experiences that would bring balance into my life. Rather than emotionally tying all my happiness to one person or endeavor, I learned that I needed to have a variety of interests in my life.

Jeffers gave an example of a woman who considered herself a good mother because she made taking care of her children her whole life. While many of you were raised to think putting our children first is a good thing, this can backfire if you use it to feel needed. If you depend on your children for emotional survival, when they grow up and go out on their own, the emptiness can be devastating.

Careers can work the same way. One of my former coworkers who made her career her whole life was devastated when she could no longer work. In spite of her doctor's insistence that she needed rest, she kept dragging herself to work. Soon she was so weak she couldn't even climb the two flights of stairs to her office. A coworker found her sitting on the bottom step and took her home. Without her job, her life was empty.

The way to avoid having this huge emptiness and despair is to create a *whole life* that looks like a grid with many compartments. Sure, your family and work will be important components of your life, but they must not be your whole life.

Here is a grid based on Jeffers' suggestion that represents my life. When I separated from my husband (and he died a year and a half later), my relationship box was full for a while when I had a boyfriend. When that relationship ended, however, my relationship box was empty again. I dated and enjoyed time with friends and family, but haven't yet filled the relationship box with a significant other, because I enjoy travel and time alone, so I did not and do not feel devastated.

CONTRIBUTION	FAMILY	WORK
HOBBY	ALONE TIME	~~RELATIONSHIP~~
TRAVEL	SPIRITUAL GROWTH	FRIENDS

When I retired from my teaching career, I certainly missed my work and my students, but I still had many other activities and interests to keep me busy and fulfilled. As a matter of fact, I replaced my work with becoming an author, speaker, and coach. Even though my relationship box still does not have a significant other in it, I know that I gave my past relationships my all and will do the same for the next relationship when it appears. Here is my whole-life grid today:

CONTRIBUTION	FAMILY	~~WORK~~ Writer, author, coach
HOBBY	ALONE TIME	~~RELATIONSHIP~~
TRAVEL	SPIRITUAL GROWTH	FRIENDS

Jeffers was quick to urge us not to think of Contribution on grand scale. We are not Martin Luther King, Jr., or Mohandas K. Gandhi. Mother Teresa, founder of the Missionaries of Charity, confirmed the importance of choosing your contribution in keeping with your own goals when she said:

> *Stay where you are. Find your own Calcutta. Find the sick, the suffering, and the lonely right there where you are—in your own homes and in your own families, in your workplaces and in your schools. You can find Calcutta*

> *all over the world, if you have the eyes to see. Everywhere, wherever ou go, you find people who are unwanted, unloved, uncared for, just rejected by society—completely forgotten, completely left alone.*

Shared by Mother Teresa with
Marie Constantin, official photographer
of Mother Teresa (http://theadvocate.com/
home/9676504-123/after-years-of-travel-with)

I have a friend whose contribution is being a foster mom to homeless kittens, and another friend who volunteers to work with homeless children who grow up living in motels. I support two charities by donating my time and energy to their events and campaigns throughout the year. Your contribution is your way of helping to make this world a better place.

Create your own whole-life grid based on Jeffers (1987) suggestions and write in the components that will ensure your physical, emotional, intellectual, and mental well-being needs are met. Your whole-life grid will be different from mine. The key to keeping your life in harmony is to give each component your all. That doesn't mean that your time or attention is evenly divided among them—just that you engage fully when you turn to the activities that make up each component.

> *One of the secrets of a happy life is continuous small treats.*
>
> —Iris Murdoch

As you attend to the activities and relationships posted on your whole-life grid, enjoy small treats and celebrate small successes. Don't wait until special occasions to say thank you and show appreciation for your life and the opportunities to expand your happiness.

4. *Be willing to get rid of the life you planned.*

> *We must be willing to get rid of the life we've planned, so as to have the life that is waiting for us. The old skin has to be shed before the new one can come.*
>
> —Joseph Campbell

Be aware that connecting the dots may or may *not* require making a major overhaul or big changes. Here are three good reasons to get rid of the life you planned:

a. *The plan no longer fits your reality.* Stylish shoes were once my weakness. Three-inch heels showed off my long legs and made me feel sexy. Even when they were uncomfortable, I tolerated the heels when they matched my outfit and brought compliments as I stepped into the room.

   But high heels no longer fit my reality. I'm

much more interested in being comfortable and care very little about what others think about my shoes. Or anything else.

Yes, I still look at high heels as I pass store windows, but now I imagine forcing the designer to wear them all day until he collapses.

b. *Your experiences and new knowledge call for a change to your plan.* When I left junior high teaching for university teaching, I scoffed at teaching in community colleges. I thought of community colleges as glorified high schools and wanted no part of a low-status institution.

Fast forward several years to the day I was choosing among three job offers. Now teaching at a community college was by far the best choice. I retired after twenty years of teaching at a community college.

Please don't cling to an old plan that no longer fits or feels good.

c. *You've run into a dead-end or detour.* I was raised as a Baptist, but as an adult I have researched many religions. I have been drawn to churches that combine Eastern and Western thought. For many years, I belonged to congregations in Religious Science, Unitarian-Universalism, and other groups that promote spiritual transformation. Eventually, however, I hit a dead-end. I felt the need for another change, but I wasn't sure what was next.

Then I went to a new church forming in my neighborhood. It was a Presbyterian church, a religion I had never investigated or considered before. I didn't even know what Presbyterians believed at first, but I was drawn to the service, the music, and the spirit of the congregation. It was also the first African-American Presbyterian church in our county. I didn't know where this was going, but for a while I took this detour and belonged to this new church.

In every one of the congregations I've joined, I engaged fully and made fulfilling contributions. None of my experiences may appeal to you, but what is important is to be true to yourself and let go of the old plan if a new one is required.

5. *Mind your legacy.* Whether you plan it or not, you will leave a legacy. It isn't unusual for people who face a terminal illness to become concerned about what memories and keepsake items they will leave behind for family and friends. But you don't have to wait for such an urgent time before you think about your legacy. I'm not talking about your funeral or memorial plans, although many find comfort in making these preparations.

We all want to believe that our lives were of some importance and that we made a difference in this world. Whether death is impending or we imagine it in the distant future, there are a number of ways to prepare the things for which we want to be remembered.

Tick tock.

Time is passing as you read this. As time passes, you leave memories in the minds and lives you touch... whether you intend to or not. How about living your life in such a way that your legacy isn't just bits and pieces of a puzzle that may fit together, but memories you chose to leave behind because they have meaning for you?

Pass on your life story and the history of your family to your children. Here are some suggestions:

> *Take photos.* And be sure to put the date on each one. You'll be amazed how difficult it is to try to remember the date of an event based on what you were wearing or what's in the background.
>
> *Keep a journal.* I have never been consistent about keeping a journal, but I have several that cover various times in my life. I've also discovered that appointment calendars and address books contain clues about your life and events through the years.
>
> *Create letters, poems, music, and art.* You don't have to be very creative to leave behind art that will be meaningful to your family and friends. When I write my Christmas poems, I'm more concerned with content and rhyme than with poetic rhythm. I enjoy writing them and everyone enjoys the annual update, sprung though my rhythm may be.
>
> *Write a book.* Some people share their

thoughts, experiences, and advice about life in their books. Maya Angelou wrote *Letters to My Daughters* to share her upbringing and life experiences with others. Even though she didn't give birth to a daughter, she had much to say to the diversity of women she saw as her daughters. Likewise, in a powerful collection of essays, Nerburn (1999) shared his thoughts, wisdom, and advice on wealth vs. poverty, possessions, loneliness vs. solitude, drugs and alcohol, tragedy and suffering, education, and more.

Make recordings of stories from your life. These can be simple MP3 files or you could have the stories transcribed into written form and disseminated—whether as audio stories or written stories or both—to loved ones.

Write your own epitaph. Some may think it's morbid, but it's an interesting exercise that forces you to sum up the meaning of your life—while you're still alive to do something about it if you wish.

In the months prior to his death, Thomas Jefferson designed his own gravestone, and wrote: "Here was buried Thomas Jefferson, Author of the Declaration of American Independence, of the Statute of Virginia for religious toleration, and Father of the University of Virginia."

Your epitaph doesn't have to be newsworthy. Few of us can lay claim to a document such as the Declaration of Independence, but we can decide how we want to be remembered.

Some epitaphs are funny. This one was found in a Georgia cemetery:

I told you I was sick!

Playing with names in a Ruidoso, New Mexico, cemetery, the epitaph read:

Here lies Johnny Yeast.
Pardon me
For not rising.

When I was in sixth grade, every Tuesday we had to recite a poem in front of class. Although we thought the poems were pretty hokey, and the concepts often didn't make sense to our young minds, we did the assignment every week. Some of those poems still pop into my head on occasion and express just the right thought for the situation. Here is one of my favorites about how to live your life knowing that you're leaving behind a legacy.

What the Heart of the Young Man Said to the Psalmist

Henry Wadsworth Longfellow

Tell me not, in mournful numbers,
Life is but an empty dream!
For the soul is dead that slumbers,
And things are not what they seem.
Life is real! Life is earnest!
And the grave is not its goal;
Dust thou art, to dust returnest,
Was not spoken of the soul.
Not enjoyment, and not sorrow,
Is our destined end or way;
But to act, that each to-morrow
Find us farther than to-day.
Art is long, and Time is fleeting,
And our hearts, though stout and brave,
Still, like muffled drums, are beating
Funeral marches to the grave.
In the world's broad field of battle,
In the bivouac of Life,
Be not like dumb, driven cattle!
Be a hero in the strife!
Trust no Future, howe'er pleasant!
Let the dead Past bury its dead!
Act, act in the living Present!
Heart within, and God o'erhead!
Lives of great men all remind us
We can make our lives sublime,

And, departing, leave behind us
Footprints on the sands of time;
Footprints, that perhaps another,
Sailing o'er life's solemn main,
A forlorn and shipwrecked brother,
Seeing, shall take heart again.
Let us, then, be up and doing,
With a heart for any fate;
Still achieving, still pursuing,
Learn to labor and to wait.

Summary

As you move toward your goals, evaluate the advice and lessons you've experienced to see what resonates with your values. When things don't go as planned, pause to see if a better plan is emerging. Be willing to change direction. Be brave enough to change your mind when it seems right for you.

We all want our lives to have meaning. We want to leave a legacy that reflects the highlights of our lives, our memories, and the family history we value. We can pass on our life story and history by taking photos, keeping a journal, creating personal correspondence, writing a book, or writing our own epitaph, among other things.

Helping others gives us gratification and contributes to our happiness. Leaving tangible memories of our lives will enhance the lives of those who come after us.

Connect your own dots. Aim for a whole life always looking for the hidden benefit in heartache and the lessons in adversity. Dedicate your life to being true, caring, and supportive of yourself. Enjoy the small victories and simple pleasures. Most of all, remember if you're not following your own dream, you're helping someone else follow theirs.

Creating your unique path will take you down many roads, and it will wind you past many people and experiences. Cherish and savor the pleasant ones and let yourself learn from the rest. There is not one way, just your way. When you discover your way and claim your joy, you'll discover that it was inside you all the time.

HAPPINESS FLASHBACK

One semester when I had to teach classes at seven in the morning, my mother gave my youngest daughter breakfast and then dropped her at school for me. After a number of weeks of eating breakfast with my mother, one weekend morning my youngest said, "Will you fix me some ones like Grandma does?"

"Ones?" I asked.

"Yes, ones. Grandma always makes me ones."

I had no idea what she was talking about, so I called my mother. "Adrienne says you fix her ones for breakfast. What is she talking about?" I asked.

"Oh." My mother immediately knew what I was talking about. "She means link sausages. She calls them ones."

AFTERWORD

A book is more than ink and paper or words delivered digitally. I hope you feel the words I've shared here are full of life and energy. They're here for you to accept and act upon. If you accept them, you will get the inspiration, direction, and ideas you need to create happiness in your life, however you define it.

When a sixty-five-year-old friend was found dead on her kitchen floor, I thought it was wonderful that she had died in action, doing one of the things she loved. I imagined that I might like to die that way, too, doing something I love.

Then, after giving it more consideration, I thought maybe the best way would be to die peacefully asleep in my own bed.

Whatever way I go, I don't want to die with my song inside me, my story untold, my trips untraveled, my love unshared, my dreams unrealized, and my purpose unfulfilled. I hope you don't either.

In a letter prefacing his book *Man and Superman: a Comedy and Philosophy*, George Bernard Shaw urged us not to waste our lives complaining that the world is not making us happy. He believed that we hold the key to living our own meaningful, joyful, and productive lives.

Instead of blaming our circumstances, he advocated changing our circumstances by making our community and world a better place, and appreciating the chance to do so. In the book *George Bernard Shaw, His Life and Works* (1911), Archibald Henderson shares this statement he heard Shaw say in Brighton in 1907:

> My life belongs to the whole community and as long as I live, it is a privilege to do for it whatsoever I can. I want to be thoroughly used up when I die, for the harder I work, the more I live. I rejoice in life for its own sake. Life is no "brief candle" to me. It is a sort of splendid torch which I have got hold of for the moment; and I want to make it burn as brightly as possible before handing it on to future generations.

If you have trouble believing that happiness is within your grasp, you're not alone. We find it so much easier and more socially acceptable to believe that some people are lucky or know a secret that escaped the rest of us.

Avoid sabotaging yourself by clinging to the popular belief that life is a game where the rules are ever-changing. Life is not a battle with a winner and a loser, nor a puzzle where the pieces never fit.

Life is a journey. To experience happiness on your

journey, you must *embrace life now*. If you can't be happy now, then you can't be happy later. "Someday" is not a day on the calendar. In our real lives there is only today, *this day*.

Happiness is not the absence of sadness, nor does being happy depend on circumstances outside ourselves. Problems, adversity, and change will always be with us. You cannot wait until the world is at peace, the economy is booming, and every hungry person is fed. As a matter of fact, the best way to help solve some of the world's problems is to create your own happiness by making your own path and claiming your own joy. In this way, you are able to contribute in some way to the solution.

Happiness is the state of mind that enables you to face your fears and setbacks, and reach within your reservoir of strength, joy, love, and peace to find purpose and meaning. Carrying out your purpose will help you and others. Being grateful will give meaning to your life and to the lives of those you help.

> *A bit of fragrance always clings to the hand that gives you roses.*
>
> —Chinese proverb

I challenge you to suspend your skepticism, open your mind to the possibility of happiness, and incorporate some of the ideas I've shared into your own life. Commit to harmonizing your family and work, finding your spiritual path, insisting on a job you love, releasing your leader within, and connecting the dots that lead to your unique life path.

Part of my life's purpose is to share this gift with you. Your gift to yourself and the world is to claim the joy you deserve so you can color your life happy.

Start now.

About the Author

Flora Brown was born in St. Louis, Missouri, and grew up in a poor segregated area. Although it was a time when many opportunities were denied African Americans, she never felt poor because her parents were hard-working and made many sacrifices. Her father was a retired foundry worker and her mother operated her own home-based beauty salon while keeping alive her love of music as the pianist and organist for the children's choir at Central Baptist Church.

Growing up in a beauty shop sparked Flora's entrepreneurial interest. She often turned crafts she learned at YWCA classes into money-making projects. Around age ten, for example, she sold her handmade potholders to the patrons of her mother's beauty shop while they sat captive under the dryer or waited their turns. From then on, she was hooked on earning money from her creative endeavors.

Around the same time, she began writing poetry about her daily life and aspirations. That's when she discovered her words could also delight, inspire, and entertain others.

But she loved school too and wanted to be a teacher. Since she couldn't decide on just one pursuit, she combined teaching, writing, and entrepreneurship with being a wife and mom.

As a graduate of USC with an M.S. in Education and a Ph.D. in Curriculum and Instruction, Flora taught junior high through university levels during her 40-year teaching career. Even while teaching, she continued to write, run a tutoring business, and serve as consultant to gift retailers. She and her husband raised four children, one of whom delighted the family with three grandchildren.

Now retired as Professor Emeritus from Fullerton College, Flora has moved into helping heart-based coaches and entrepreneurs write, market, and publish lead-generating, client-attracting, and life-transforming books. People worldwide subscribe to her newsletters and blogs and learn from her classes and tutorials. Learn more at http://florabrown.com.

Color Your Life Happy: Create Your Unique Path and Claim the Joy You Deserve, is her eleventh book. Be sure to leave an honest review of this book and check out her other books at http://www.amazon.com/author/florabrown.

Flora confesses to being a coffee snob who loves music from Ray Charles to Vivaldi and has an unhealthy love of British murder mysteries (especially Sherlock Holmes). She plans to visit every continent and many major countries, getting to know the food, customs, and locals. (She has one continent to go.)

REFERENCES

Beck, M. (2001). *Finding your own North Star: Claiming the life you were meant to live.* New York: Three Rivers Press.

Bouchard, T., Lykken, D., McGue, M., Segal, N., & Tellegen, A. (1990). Sources of human psychological differences: The Minnesota study of twins reared apart. *Science, 250*(4978), 223–28. Retrieved from http://web.missouri.edu/~segerti/1000H/Bouchard.pdf

Bradley, S. (2000). *Sudden money: Managing a financial windfall.* New Jersey: Wiley.

Breathnach, S. B. (2009). *Simple abundance: A daybook of comfort and joy.* New York: Grand Central Publishing.

Brickman, P., & Campbell, D. (1971). Hedonic relativism and planning the good society. In M. H. Apley (Ed.), *Adaptation-level theory: A symposium* (pp. 287–302). Waltham, MA: Academic Press.

Bush, A. D. (2011). *Shortcuts to inner peace: 70 simple paths to everyday serenity.* New York: Berkley Publishing Group.

Csikszentmihalyi, M. (1990). *Flow.* New York: Harper Collins Publishers.

Cousins, N. (1979). *Anatomy of an illness.* New York: W. W. Norton & Company.

Covey, S. (2013). *The seven habits of highly effective people.* New York: Simon and Schuster.

Dirksen, K. (2011, March 8). *Happiness research ranks commuting low: One-hour commute cuts your social life by 10 percent* [Web log post]. Retrieved from http://www.huffingtonpost.com/kirsten-dirksen/happiness-research-ranks-_b_829591.html

Dyer, W. (2005). *The power of intention.* Carlsbad, CA: Hay House.

Ekman, P., Davidson, R., & Friesen, W. (1990, February). The Duchenne smile: Emotional expression and brain physiology: II. *Journal of Personality and Social Psychology, 58*(2), 342–353.

Emmons, R. (2007). *Thanks: How the new science of gratitude can make you happier.* New York: Houghton Mifflin.

Fair, M. (2013). *Tilt: 7 Solutions to be a guilt-free working mom*. Lawrenceville, GA: Pacochel Press.

Frankl, V. (2006). *Man's search for meaning*. Boston: Beacon Press.

Gibson, B., & Sanbonmatsu, D. (2004, February). Optimism, pessimism, and gambling: The downside of optimism. *Personality and Social Psychology Bulletin*, *3*(2), 149–160. doi:10.1177/0146167203259929.

Gilbert, D. (2005). *Stumbling on happiness*. New York: Vintage Books.

Gill, M. (2007). *How Starbucks saved my life: A son of privilege learns to live like everyone else*. New York: Gotham.

Godin, S. (2007). *The dip*. New York: Portfolio.

Goodheart, A. (1994). *Laughter therapy: How to laugh about everything in your life that isn't really funny*. Santa Barbara, CA: Less Stress Press.

Gore, A. (2010). *Bluebird: Women and the new psychology of happiness*. New York: Farrar, Straus and Giroux

Grant, K. (2013, June 30). Americans hate their jobs even with perks [Web log post]. Retrieved from http://www.usatoday.com/story/money/business/2013/06/30/americans-hate-jobs-office-perks/2457089/

Green, Penelope. (2008, January 31). The slow life picks up speed. Retrieved from http://www.nytimes.com/2008/01/31/garden/31slow.html

Gruber, J. (2011). Happiness has a dark side. Retrieved from http://www.medicalnewstoday.com/releases/225526.php

Haidt, J. (2006). *The happiness hypothesis*. Boston, MA: Basic Books.

Holder, M., Coleman, B., & Wallace, J. (2010, April). Spirituality, religiousness, and happiness in children aged 8–12 years. *Journal of Happiness Studies, 11*(2), 131–150.

Honore, C. (2005). *In praise of slowness: Challenging the cult of speed.* New York: Harper One.

Hsieh, T. (2013). *Delivering happiness: A path to profits, passion and purpose.* New York: Grand Central Publishing.

Iacoboni, M. (2009). Mirroring people: The science of empathy and how we connect to others. New York: Picador.

Inglehart, R., Foa, R., Peterson, C., & Welzel, C. (2008, July). Development, freedom and rising happiness (1981–2007).*PerspectivesonPsychologicalScience*,*3*(5), 264–285. doi:10.1111/j.1745-6924.2008.00078.x

Jeffers, S. (1987). *Feel the fear and do it anyway.* New York: Ballantine Books.

Kaplan, R., & Kaplan, S. (1989). *The experience of nature: A psychological perspective.* New York: Cambridge University Press.

Kashdan, T., & Biswas-Diener, R. (2014). *The upside of your dark side: Why being your whole self—not just your "good self"—drives success and fulfillment.* New York: Hudson Street Press.

Katie, B. (2003). *Loving what is: Four questions that can change your life.* New York: Three Rivers Press.

Kushner, H. S. (2004). *When bad things happen to good people.* New York: Knopf Doubleday Publishing Group

Lama, D., & Cutler, H. (2009). *The art of happiness in a troubled world.* New York: Three Rivers Press.

Lipton, B. (2007). *The biology of belief: Unleashing the power of consciousness, matter and miracles.* Carlsbad, CA: Hay House.

Marsh, S. (2012). *From freeways to flip flops: A family's year of gutsy living on a tropical island.* Lake Forest, California: Gutsy Publications.

McConnell, A., Brown, C., Shoda, T., Stayton, L., & Martin, C. (2011, December). Friends with benefits: On the positive consequences of pet ownership. *Journal of Personality and Social Psychology, 101*(6), 1239–1252.

Neill, M. (2007, August 31). Have an average day: Enjoying the ordinary is extraordinary [Web log post]. Retrieved from http://www.catalystmagazine.net/component/k2/item/345-genius-catalyst-have-an-average-day

Nerburn, K. (1999). *Letters to my son: A father's wisdom on manhood, life and love.* Novato, CA: New World Library.

Norem, J. (2002). *The positive power of negative thinking.* New York: Basic Books.

Pavlina, S. (2006, January 27). Beyond self-delusional positive thinking [Web log post]. Retrieved from http://www.stevepavlina.com/blog/2006/01/beyond-self-delusional positive-thinking/

Pressman, S., & Kraft, T. (2012, October 31). Grin and bear it: The influence of manipulated facial expression on the stress response. *Psychological Science,* 23(11), 1372–1378.

Price, M. (2009). *Fearless thinking.* Harrison, NY: BCH Fulfillment and Distribution.

Putnam, R. D. (2000) *Bowling alone: The collapse and revival of American community*. New York: Simon & Schuster, 2000.

Ritchey, N. (2012, June 15). Kaizen: Accomplishing big goals with tiny steps [Web log post]. Retrieved from http://psychologyofwellbeing.com/201206/kaizen-accomplishing-big-goals-with-tiny-steps.html

Roth, G. (2011, May 16). The spiritual power of dance [Web log post]. Retrieved from http://www.huffingtonpost.com/gabrielle-roth/spirituality-dance_b_862226.html

Rubin, G. (2009). *The happiness project: Or why I spent a year trying to sing in the morning, clean my closets, fight right, read Aristotle, and generally have more fun*. New York: Harper Collins.

Rudd, M., Aaker, J., & Vohs, K. (2012, July 19). Awe expands people's perception of time, alters decision making, and enhances well-being. *Psychological Science. doi: 10.1177/0956797612438731.*

Seligman, M. (2011). *Learned optimism: How to change your mind and your life*. New York: Vintage.

Seligman, M. (2007). *What you can change and what you can't*. New York: Vintage.

Sher, B. (2007). *Refuse to choose*. Emmaus, PA: Rodale Books.

Siegel, B. (1998). *Love, medicine and miracle*. New York: William Morrow.

Simms, S. (2011, December 19). The last thought principle [Web log post]. Retrieved from https://stevesimms.wordpress.com/2011/12/19/the-last-thought-principle/

Smith, L. M. (2012). *How to write heartfelt letters to treasure: For special occasions and occasions made special*. Yorba Linda, CA: All My Best.

St. John, N. (2014). *Afformations: The miracle of positive self-talk*. Carlsbad, CA: Hay House.

Stutzer, A., & Frey, B. (2004, August). *Stress that doesn't pay: The commuting paradox*. IZA DP No. 1278. Retrieved from http://ftp.iza.org/dp1278.pdf

Suzuki, S. (1999). *Nurtured by love: The classic approach to talent education* (2nd ed.). New York: Amereon Ltd.

Thoreau, H. D. (2013). *Walden*. New York: Empire Books.

Vujicic, N. (2010). *Life without limbs: Inspiration for a ridiculously good life*. Colorado Springs, CO: WaterBrook Press.

Wahls, T. (2010). *Minding my mitochondria: How I overcame secondary progressive multiple sclerosis (MS) and got out of my wheelchair* (2nd ed.). Iowa City, IA: TZ Press.

Welch, S. (2009). *10-10-10: A life transforming idea.* New York: Scribner.

INDEX

A

D

L

Q

R

T

X

Y

Z

Made in the USA
San Bernardino, CA
10 March 2016